ABOUT THE AUTHOR

Martin is a freelance marketing consultant, trainer, facilitator, public speaker and writer. He works with a wide variety of brand owners and marketing agencies, providing advice on business, brand and communications planning and the strategic application of social media. He has led award-winning advertising, media, PR and sponsorship teams and has been one of the pioneers of integrated brand and communications planning. His first book, *Crowd Surfing*, which he co-wrote with David Brain, was published in 2008.

Martin is a non-executive director of Sport England and the Commonwealth Games Council for England and is also a Fellow of the Royal Society for the encouragement of Arts, Manufactures and Commerce (RSA) and a member of the Marketing Society. He remains hopeful of a first Welsh rugby cap, although recognizes that time may be running out.

He blogs at www.crowdsurfing.net
and tweets at @crowdsurfing

'*A very large oak was uprooted by the wind and thrown across a stream. It fell among some reeds, which it thus addressed: 'I wonder how you, who are so light and weak, are not entirely crushed by these strong winds.' They replied, 'You fight and contend with the wind, and consequently you are destroyed; while we on the contrary bend before the least breath of air, and therefore remain unbroken and escape.'*

Aesop, *The Oak and the Reed*,
translated by George Fyler Townsend*

---

* Internet Classics Archive, MIT.

Loose

The Future of Business is Letting Go

martin thomas

headline
business plus

First published in 2011
by HEADLINE PUBLISHING GROUP

Cataloguing in Publication Data is available from the British Library

ISBN 978 0 7553 6155 7

Typeset in Caslon by Avon DataSet Ltd, Bidford-on-Avon, Warwickshire

Printed in the UK by CPI Mackays, Chatham, ME5 8TD

Headline's policy is to use papers that are natural, renewable and
recyclable products and made from wood grown in sustainable forests.
The logging and manufacturing processes are expected to conform to
the environmental regulations of the country of origin.

HEADLINE PUBLISHING GROUP
An Hachette UK Company
338 Euston Road
London NW1 3BH

www.headline.co.uk
www.hachette.co.uk

The British poet Simon Armitage, in his memoirs *Gig: The life and times of a rock-star fantasist*, recalls returning to his home town and finding a copy of one of his books in the bargain bin of a second-hand bookshop. It was inscribed, in his own handwriting, 'To Mum and Dad'.

I dedicate this to my parents – aka Tony and Joan – in the hope that it will not find its way into a Warwickshire jumble sale any time soon.

This book is largely inspired by conversations I had following the publication of my first book, which I co-wrote with Edelman's David Brain in 2008. David continued to be a great source of ideas, anecdotes and quotes, as were the always enthusiastic David Butter, Robert Campbell at Beta, Christian Barnett and Stephen Bell at CPB, Alex Batchelor and John Kearon at BrainJuicer, Dominic Stinton at VCCP, Alan Mitchell at Ctrl-shift, Peter Fisk, Tom Rowley at Pipeline, Ivan Pollard, Richard Brown at Cognosis, Robert Phillips at Edelman, James Thellusson at Glasshouse, Richard Rawlins at Finn, Jane Ferguson and Marshall Dawson. I would also like to thank my agent (I have always wanted to say that), Simon Benham at MayerBenham and John Moseley at Headline, who thankfully saw something in my loosely formed idea. Finally and most importantly, I would like to thank the three most important people in my life, Alison, Daniel and Louis, who lived through the ups and downs of the writing process, contributed many ideas and never once suggested that I should get a proper job. This book is for all of you.

CONTENTS

CHAPTER 1

INTRODUCTION

Bᴇʟɢɪᴀɴ ᴛʀᴀꜰꜰɪᴄ ᴘʟᴀɴɴᴇʀ Hans Monderman was not afraid to challenge conventional thinking. When we drive our cars we are used to travelling within clearly demarcated lanes and expect our movements to be controlled by an array of signs and traffic lights. Motorists, cyclists and pedestrians are kept to separate parts of the highway. We find comfort in order. Monderman challenged this convention. He argued that traffic lights, signs and road markings actually made roads less safe because they took away people's ability to think for themselves and that by removing them, motorists, cyclists and pedestrians would be encouraged to co-exist more happily and safely. He was a leader of the Shared Space movement, also described as 'designing for negotiation', which is beginning to find more and more advocates in traffic management departments around the world. He pioneered his thinking in the Dutch town of Drachten, where 12 of the 15 sets of traffic lights were removed. The results were remarkable. The number of accidents in Drachten fell from an average of 8.3 per year in 2003 to just one a year in 2004 and 2005. There are still the occasional collisions, but Monderman, in his typically contrarian style, saw these as a good thing: 'We want small accidents, in order

to prevent serious ones in which people get hurt.'[1] Simon
Jenkins, writing in the *Guardian*, quipped that 'the chief
danger [on the roads in Drachten] is from crowds of foreign
experts watching incredulously as traffic merges with
pedestrians and separates, unaided by robots'.[2]

The Shared Space concept is safer because, to its users, it
appears (paradoxically) to be more dangerous. Monderman
argued that it required the driver to take responsibility for
their own risk, rather than abdicate responsibility to government or other forms of authority. It also challenges the broadly
accepted hierarchy on our streets, forcing motorists to negotiate
with other road users rather than assume that they always
have priority. Drivers entering a shared space zone tend to
slow down and start responding directly to the behaviour of
other road users, rather than slavishly taking direction from
signs and traffic lights. For example, there is evidence that
drivers are more likely to slow down if they see children
actually playing in the street, than if they simply see a sign
saying 'Danger Children'. Eye contact with fellow road users
suddenly becomes more important and drivers start taking
more interest in what is happening around them than the DJ's
chatter on the car radio. Monderman compared his philosophy
of traffic management to the way that skaters behave on a
crowded ice rink: 'Skaters work out things for themselves and
it works wonderfully well. I am not an anarchist, but I don't
like rules which are ineffective and street furniture tells people
how to behave.'[3]

Monderman, who died in 2008, aged only 62, wasn't a

---

[1] Quoted in *Daily Telegraph*, 4 November 2006.
[2] *Guardian*, 29 February 2008.
[3] Quoted in *Daily Telegraph*, 4 November 2006.

management guru or a highly paid business consultant, but he understood human behaviour and, most importantly, was prepared to question our naive faith in the necessity of structure and clearly defined boundaries. He was prepared to challenge 'rules which are ineffective', even if this brought him into conflict with received wisdom. His philosophy has been enthusiastically taken up by many traffic-management experts around the world, including Ben Hamilton-Baillie in the UK, whose Bristol-based practice has worked on a large number of shared space schemes. These have included a project in the Royal Borough of Kensington and Chelsea, in which the removal of railings and many of the signs and posts cluttering the borough's streets reduced the number of pedestrian casualties by three times the London average. According to Hamilton-Baillie, railings, despite appearing to protect pedestrians from the onrushing traffic, actually 'encourage people on both sides [of them] to pay less attention to each other, which is potentially dangerous'.[4]

The shared space concept does have its critics and even advocates, such as Hamilton-Baillie, accept that it can only work in the right locations. But it has forced the traffic-management and planning experts to revisit many of their widely held beliefs. Graeme Swinburne, Kensington's director of transport, spoke for many of his peers when admitting that 'Engineers tend to be risk-averse; these guidelines [issued by the Institution of Civil Engineers to support the principle of removing railings] have reassured us that we can challenge the established thinking.'[5] Traffic management has been the epitome of tight thinking, but the increased willingness to

---

[4] *The Times*, 8 April 2006.
[5] *The Times*, 8 April 2006.

consider shared space ideas suggests that things are beginning to loosen up. Even the government has been forced to admit recently that speed cameras may not be as effective in reducing serious accidents as it had previously claimed. Some reports have gone so far as to suggest that the rate of decline in the number of accidents actually slowed down after the intro-duction of cameras.[6]

Pope Benedict XVI is not a name you expect to find in business books. Despite what was generally considered to be a successful visit to the UK, he remains mired in the ongoing controversy about the church's handling of child-abuse allegations. Like all of his predecessors he is often accused of leading an institution that struggles to adapt to the modern world. Nevertheless, there are signs that things are loosening up in the Vatican, particularly when it comes to its willingness to embrace new media technologies. The Pope may not be the most charismatic communicator, but his YouTube broadcasts, translated into 27 languages, are an interesting attempt to connect him with what he describes as the global digital generation, even if, unlike Barack Obama, his message is more a case of 'No you can't', rather than 'Yes you can'. He was the first major religious leader to call for the use of social media to engage the faithful and recruit new converts. In a speech on the role of digital communications to mark the 44th World Communications Day,[7] he called upon the priesthood to 'make astute use of the unique possibilities

---

[6] *Speeding Fines*: report commissioned by the Taxpayers' Alliance and Drivers' Alliance, published 9 July 2010.

[7] Speech given to mark the 44th World Communications Day – 'The Priest and Pastoral Ministry in a Digital World: New Media at the Service of the Word', 16 May 2010.

offered by modern communications' and challenged them to use 'the latest generation of audiovisual resources (images, videos, animated features, blogs, websites) which, alongside traditional means, can open up broad new vistas for dialogue, evangelization and catechesis'.

The views expressed by the man responsible for managing the Pope's public relations, Father Federico Lombardi, are equally refreshing. Like the Pope, Lombardi has been accused of being out of touch with contemporary attitudes, but in a speech in London he sounded like a model new age marketer, claiming that, 'In a world such as ours, we would be deluding ourselves if we thought that communication can always be controlled, or that it can always be conducted smoothly and as a matter of course.' He then went on to say that, 'It is a mistake to think we ought to avoid debate', which is a pretty bold statement coming from an institution wedded historically to certainty and the primacy of its viewpoint. Debating Church doctrine would have landed you in front of the Inquisition during an earlier age. Some religious commentators have described how the Church's willingness to embrace new media – and the new expectations that come with it – could be as significant as its willingness to embrace Gutenberg's printing press in the 1450s. The rapid adoption of the printing press in Europe's intellectual centres during the second half of the fifteenth century – which could be considered the first information revolution – forced the Church to respond to new ideas and openly debate fundamental parts of its doctrine. It ultimately played a key role in the emergence of the Protestant Reformation. The Church's use of social media is unlikely to have such profound effects, but there are signs that it is encouraging a new spirit of openness and dialogue, particularly at a local level, where many clergy and congregations have enthusiastically embraced the Pope's call to leverage the power of modern communications techniques. The Catholic Church simply doesn't have the option, if it is to truly embrace these new media channels, of not allowing debate or the occasional disagreement.

Staying within the world of religion, one of the defining ideological battles of the 21st century has been between Islamic fundamentalism and Western liberalism. But this is not simply a battle between rival theologies. We are also witnessing the clash of two very different organizational models – that of the state-controlled intelligence and military services and the loose, cellular structure of Al-Qaeda. Writing in the *Middle East Quarterly*, defence experts Daveed Gartenstein-Ross and Kyle Dabruzzi, described the merits of this structure: 'Bureaucratic intelligence agencies have trouble keeping up with cells that are disconnected and on the move, making it almost impossible to uproot an entire decentralized network. Regional terrorist groups can also act with greater spontaneity without the need to coordinate their operations through hierarchical channels.'[8]

In many respects, Al-Qaeda is the perfect loose organizational model for the modern world, which is somewhat ironic when you consider how much of its theology and political language sounds as though it comes from the Middle Ages. Douglas Frantz, in the *Los Angeles Times*, described it as 'more of an ideology than an organization'.[9] It adheres to a broad set of principles and objectives determined by a small leadership team, with Osama Bin-Laden at its head, but it operates

---

[8] Daveed Gartenstein-Ross and Kyle Dabruzzi, 'Is Al-Qaeda's Central Leadership Still Relevant?', *Middle East Quarterly*, Spring 2008.
[9] *Los Angeles Times*, 26 September 2004.

through a complex network of semi-autonomous units or cells. Decision-making is dispersed and there are few connections between the different cells. It has also evolved its behaviour, if not its theology, in response to changing circumstances. US Secretary of State Hillary Clinton has described how it has become 'more creative, more flexible and more agile',[10] which is why, despite the military and financial muscle of the United States and its partners, Al-Qaeda continues to threaten our global security.

In contrast, the CIA, despite all of its technological and intellectual firepower, appears to be struggling to come to terms with the new world. In a Google-sponsored panel discussion, CIA analyst Sean Dennehy said that the organization was finding it a challenge to adapt to the idea of sharing information through blogs and social networks and commented that, 'Trying to implement these tools in the intelligence community is basically like telling people that their parents raised them wrong.'[11] Speaking at the same event, Lt Col. Patrick Michaelis, one of the people responsible for helping to develop the US Army's online forum, which enables soldiers to share intelligence while in combat, admitted that, 'In essence we're still culturally a hierarchy when it comes to transferring knowledge and data. It is always a challenge to connect the bottom to the top.'

The merits of the loose, decentralized Al-Qaeda structure, and, in particular, its ability to survive frequent attempts to destroy it, are not lost on Andrew Haldane, Executive Director for Financial Stability at the Bank of England. He has described how the global banking industry would do well to copy the

---

[10] Interviewed on CNN's *State of the Union*, 7 February 2010.
[11] Quoted by *Brand Republic*, 16 June 2009.

terrorist group's modular structure if it is to avoid future crises: 'A series of decentralised cells, loosely bonded, make infiltration of the entire Al-Qaeda network extremely unlikely. If any one cell is incapacitated, the likelihood of this undermining the operations of other cells is severely reduced. That, of course, is precisely why Al-Qaeda has chosen this organisational form. Al-Qaeda is a prime example of modularity and its effects in strengthening systemic resilience.'[12] Haldane made these remarks in a speech given in Hong Kong. I am not sure they would have gone down so well on Wall Street, but it underlines how Al-Qaeda is defined as much by its organizational model as by its theology.

The future lies with the contrarian theories of Monderman and the newly discovered laissez-faire attitudes expressed by Lombardi in the Vatican – which I would characterize as loose thinking – combined with the type of loose organizational model deployed by Al-Qaeda. I am conscious that 'loose' is a challenging word and comes with many negative connotations. For many business experts it appears to espouse chaos rather than structure, solid organization and the benefit of accumulated knowledge. It sounds unprofessional and dangerously informal; an excuse to avoid due process, careful analysis and rigorous thought. It may be fine for a freewheeling, technology start-up in Silicon Valley, but how can it make sense for major corporations, employing tens of thousands of people and responsible for satisfying the demands of millions of global customers, or for governments trying to balance debt reduction with escalating social problems? A business such as Google, bank-rolled by vast advertising revenues, can espouse the concept

---

[12] Speaking at the Institute of Regulation & Risk, North Asia (IRRNA), in Hong Kong, 30 March 2010.

of 'thriving on the edge of chaos',[13] indulge the creative whims of its employees and talk about the importance of failure as a learning process, but how many other businesses can afford this luxury? By the time you reach the end of this book, my hope is that this question no longer applies. By describing how looser ways of thinking and operating are beginning to pervade even the largest and most complex institutions, from global corporations to government departments, my aim is to give you the confidence and the ammunition to help you and your colleagues loosen up.

Agility, flexibility, a willingness to exercise judgement and an ability to improvise will become the defining characteristics of successful institutions in the next decades. So fight the instinct to solve every problem through rules and regulations. Ask yourself whether the decision to impose new compliance and auditing procedures is really reflecting a lack of trust in your workforce. Recognize the limitations of long-term planning and the painfully slow nature of most internal decision-making processes. Embrace the need to operate in real time and make the organizational and cultural changes necessary to help you achieve it. Invest in building a strong, self-sustaining organizational culture rather than in yet more process and bureaucracy. The future is loose, messy and chaotic: I hope you'll embrace it.

---

[13] Description of Google used by *Fortune* magazine's Adam Lashinsky (2 October 2006).

1.1 THE NEW AGE OF LOOSE AND WHY TIGHT DOESN'T WORK

'We must embrace a model of leadership that is loose, open and perpetually innovative.'

Tom Peters[14]

The need to adopt a looser or more flexible approach to the management of institutions is not a new idea. It has has been championed by many leading business thinkers, from Rosabeth Moss Kanter in *When Giants Learn to Dance* to Richard Pascale in *Surfing the Edge of Chaos*. As far back as 1959, Charles Lindblom was challenging the primacy of rational thinking in his oxymoronic article, 'The Science of "Muddling Through"'. Tom Peters, the business author and self-proclaimed professional agitator[15] has virtually made a career of it. His seminal book, *In Search of Excellence*,[16] which he co-wrote with Robert Waterman in 1982, was largely inspired by a desire to prove that the highly systematized approach, adopted by most corporations at the time, was counterproductive and that there was a need to free business from what he termed 'the tyranny of the bean counters'.

The ideas remain the same, but I would argue that the circumstances in which we now live have made them even more relevant. New patterns of consumer behaviour and changing expectations, new technology, combined with a bewilderingly complex social, cultural, economic, political and

---

[14] Tom Peters, *Re-imagine: Business Excellence in a Disruptive Age*, Dorling Kindersley, 2003.

[15] www.tompeters.com

[16] Tom Peters and Robert H. Waterman, *In Search of Excellence*, Profile Business, 2004.

environmental landscape, make loose thinking and working more important than ever. Centralized, hierarchical systems made sense in a world in which information and knowledge were relatively scarce commodities and could be tightly controlled, but the decentralization of knowledge, brought about by the inexorable rise of the internet, combined with a collapse of trust in traditional sources of authority and expertise, legitimizes the creation of flatter, decentralized operational models. In a recent survey of UK-based human resources professionals, only 35 per cent believed that the traditional command-and-control model of leadership would prevail in their organizations over the next five years, but to highlight how far most businesses have to travel, 85 per cent admitted that traditional, hierarchical forms of leadership continued to dominate their organizations.[17] Rapidly changing customer expectations are also forcing institutions to operate and respond in real time, placing a premium on agility, flexibility and an ability to improvise. Longer-term planning and cautious, careful deliberation are increasingly becoming luxuries that few organizations can afford.

TIGHT DOESN'T WORK

The other part of my argument is that tight – the antithesis of loose – while being superficially attractive and comforting, doesn't work and that the biggest weakness of most institutions is the illusion or possibly the delusion of being in control. We witness the control delusion in business leaders, who would

---

[17] 'Head office of the future', *HR Magazine*, October 2009.

rather issue a set of formal rules, and pretend that they are being adhered to, than put the time and effort into creating a culture in which people behave in the right way. It affects politicians, who regard the imposition of new legislation as the answer to all of society's problems. The deficiencies of tight thinking can also be seen in the paralysis of analysis that affects so many business decision-makers, who find comfort in the accumulation of vast amounts of market and customer data, but are then so overwhelmed that they are incapable of making any decisions. This corporate tendency was memorably highlighted by Ross Perot during his long drawn-out dispute with the senior management team at General Motors: 'I come from an environment where, if you see a snake, you kill it. At GM, if you see a snake, the first thing you do is go hire a consultant on snakes. Then you get a committee on snakes, and then you discuss it for a couple of years. The most likely course of action is— nothing. You figure, the snake hasn't bitten anybody yet, so you just let him crawl around on the factory floor. We need to build an environment where the first guy who sees the snake kills it.'[18]

In the public sector, tight thinking manifests itself in the use of targets to measure the performance of our schools, hospitals and other public services. All too often this simply results in the distortion of priorities: schools focus on softer, less academic subject areas and concentrate their efforts on pupils that will make a difference to the exam results (typically those just below the pass grade), rather than pupils at the top and bottom of the pile; hospitals manipulate waiting lists and start prioritizing quick and easy operations, rather than the

---

[18] *Fortune* magazine, 15 February 1988.

more difficult ones. David Boyle, in his highly influential book, *The Tyranny of Numbers*,[19] quotes business psychologist John Seddon: 'People do what you count, not necessarily what counts,' which echoes the famous sign hanging on the wall in Einstein's office in Princeton: 'Not everything that counts can be counted and not everything that can be counted counts.'

It is said that it takes a mere 18 months before the people in any organization work out the best way to manipulate or 'game' a target-based system, whether it governs the allocation of healthcare funding, a ranking in a government-backed league table or decisions about bankers' bonuses. After this time the system starts subverting itself, delivering a set of outcomes completely different to those that were intended and, all too often, the numbers that are being counted become more important than the behavioural change that the organization is trying to deliver. Smart managers know this, so they regularly adjust the targets and the success criteria used to measure them, but most of the time the people responsible for creating the systems and setting the targets cling to a faith in the validity and integrity of their tight, empirical world. They seem happy to remain in a state of blissful ignorance. This appears to have been a fundamental weakness within the world's leading financial institutions in the build-up to the global banking crisis. The senior directors running the world's leading financial institutions knew that their target-based culture was encouraging people to take unnecessary risks and put their own narrow interests ahead of those of their employers, but they appeared to have suffered from a case of collective myopia.

---

[19] David Boyle, *The Tyranny of Numbers: Why counting can't make us happy*, Flamingo, 2001.

A single-minded focus on numbers and targets also shifts the source of expertise and investment, particularly in our public institutions, from the front-line practitioner – the teacher or the surgeon – to the measurer of their performance – the auditors, accountants and managers: hence the growth of the back-office or managerial function in most public bodies. This almost certainly explains why the number of managers in the National Health Service in England increased by nearly 12 per cent in 2009, more than five times the rate at which qualified nurses were recruited,[20] and also why, according to the Chief Inspector of Constabulary, Sir Dennis O'Connor, only 13 per cent of police and community support officers are actually walking the beat.[21]

The recent decision by the UK's coalition government to place spending decisions in the hands of GPs and to decapitate the top tier of NHS managers by abolishing Primary Care Trusts and strategic health authorities, represents a bold – their opponents would say a foolhardy – attempt to address this issue. It has also pledged to scrap top-down targets in both health and education and evolve the NHS from a state-funded monopoly into a looser social-enterprise model. It will be interesting to observe how it manages to balance the removal of targets with the continuous demand to demonstrate accountability and efficiency, especially during a time of rapidly shrinking public finances. I sit on the board of a government quango and see at first hand the pressures on public institutions to account for every penny of public money that is spent. It is expensive to put in place the necessary auditing and compliance procedures and invest in tracking

---

[20] NHS Information Centre Study (published March 2010).
[21] Quoted in the *Guardian*, 21 July 2010.

research to measure whether desired behavioural changes have been achieved, but, given the demands of the National Audit Office and the scrutiny of the media, we are left with little alternative.

There have also been inconsistencies in the coalition's approach. Its commitment to the virtues of decentralization and rolling back the power of the state – as part of David Cameron's Big Society vision to redistribute power from 'the elite in Whitehall to the man and woman on the street'[22] – is not reflected in the decision to strip local educational authorities of their power over new academy schools, which will report directly to the Education Secretary. The government's plans for a new form of national service for 16-year-old school leavers is also based on a centralized, top-down model and has been criticized by many of the existing voluntary organizations working in the youth sector for not harnessing their specialist expertise. Most governments appear to start out with a declared commitment to the decentralization of decision-making, but a more authoritarian, centralizing instinct starts taking hold as frustration grows with the slow pace of change and the media and public start demanding that 'something must be done'. It will be interesting to see how long the coalition can stick with its looser principles before it reverts to a more centralized, autocratic mode.

We have already started to see this, to some extent, with calls to impose tougher legislative controls on the sale of alcohol, five years after the relaxation of the licensing laws. The original liberalization was intended to herald the emergence of a more relaxed, continental-style of drinking, although for

---

[22] David Cameron's Big Society launch speech 19 July 2010.

many bar owners, it simply created an opportunity for 24-hour opening. It is hardly surprising that the desired behavioural change has yet to take place – as a visit to one of our towns and cities on a Friday or Saturday night would testify – but expecting Britain's deep-seated cultural attitudes to alcohol to change within such a short period of time was always going to be unrealistic. The emergency services and media have understandably demanded that the government acts to tackle the 'Binge Britain' effect – the *Daily Mail* has called for 'a concerted fightback against the misery inflicted by Labour's liberalisation of drinking laws'[23] and described 'the social catastrophe'[24] created by a flood of cheap alcohol – conveniently forgetting that serious, alcohol-related problems predated the original decision to change the laws. There are undeniably flaws in the current system – it was never intended to provide 24-hour drinking and the price of alcohol is almost certainly too cheap – but the imposition of tighter legislation has rarely been effective in changing social behaviour.

THE DANGEROUS ILLUSION OF SIMPLICITY

As David Cameron and his new colleagues in government are discovering, the world is chaotic and confusing. Confucius may have declared that 'Life is really simple but we insist on making it complicated', but he wasn't trying to run a large organization in a highly competitive market and facing the unrelenting scrutiny of shareholders, stakeholders, activists,

---

[23] *Daily Mail*, 1 October 2009.
[24] *Daily Mail*, 20 January 2010.

employees and legislators. Our understanding of the world is not enhanced through the oversimplification of complexity or illusory faith in some artificially imposed sense of order. This is one of the key conclusions made by Stephen Chan, Professor of International Relations at the University of London's School of Oriental and African Studies. In his book *The End of Certainty*,[25] he argues that the oversimplified, Western perspective on what is, in reality, a highly complex and diverse world, lies at the heart of the failing of international politics. Harvard University's Robert Kegan made a similar point in the build-up to the 2008 US presidential election, when issuing his own situations vacant ad in *USA Today*: 'Wanted: A president with a complex mind. For as we've learned the hard way, tough issues can rarely be solved with black-and-white thinking. In the world, nothing is that simple.'[26] This was an obvious attack on the perceived limitations of George W. Bush's apparently simplistic world view. Barack Obama clearly fits the job description of someone with a 'complex mind', displaying a much more nuanced understanding of the complexities of international politics, whether talking about the shared values underpinning Christianity and Islam, or the need to form a new (post-Cold War) relationship with Russia. Awarding him the 2009 Nobel Peace Prize for 'his extraordinary efforts to strengthen international diplomacy and co-operation between peoples'[27] may have been a case of jumping the gun, for someone who has yet to deliver any tangible foreign policy achievements, but it underlined the hope that resides in

---

[25] Stephen Chan, *The End of Certainty: Towards a new internationalism*, Zed Books, 2010.
[26] *USA Today*, 13 June 2007.
[27] Statement of the Nobel Committee, 2009.

Obama's skills as an internationalist. Whether he proves to be more successful than George W. will largely depend on his ability to take Middle America (not exactly renowned for its willingness to embrace ambiguity and complexity) with him.

Professor Chan is also pretty damning about the lack of intellectual and philosophical tradition in modern Britain and our politicians' unwillingness to debate complex issues, suggesting that, 'Three decades of dogged soundbite phrase-ologies of both Thatcherism and Blairism have made debate a contest between assertions of certainty.'[28] He believes it essential that we talk about how the world really is – in all of its mess and ambiguity – rather than how we wish it would be. His views are echoed by Don Norman, described by *Business Week* as 'one of the world's most influential designers'. He has argued that 'simplicity is highly overrated' and that 'People prefer complex things. If it's too simple, it gets boring'. In his book *Living with Complexity*,[29] he celebrates complexity in pro-duct design as a good thing and necessary, because our lives are complex and therefore the tools we use to help us must reflect this reality: 'Complexity can be good, leading to a rich, satisfying life, filled with rich, satisfying experiences.'[30] But before he can be accused of advocating consumer-unfriendly design solutions, Norman makes the very important distinction between things that are complex and those that are complicated, suggesting that: 'We must distinguish complexity from con-fusion, perplexity and unintelligibility. The goal is complexity with order, lucidity and understanding.' His view is very different from that of Edward de Bono, the lateral-thinking

---

[28] www.theendofcertainty.com
[29] Donald A. Norman, *Living with Complexity*, MIT Press, 2010.
[30] Interview at North Western University.

guru, who argues that, 'Dealing with complexity is an inefficient and unnecessary waste of time, attention and mental energy. There is never any justification for things being complex when they could be simple.'[31] I tend to concur with Norman's view of the world. We don't need things to be simple, when the reality is complicated, but we do need things to be understandable. Making something deceptively simple is not as valuable as providing a clear and coherent narrative through a complex reality.

There is an adage in political circles when trying to explain complex issues to a disengaged electorate or journalists looking for a soundbite: 'Do you want the simple lie or the complicated truth?' All too often we appear willing to accept the simple lie – that economic markets are innately efficient and driven by rational thinking; that putting more people in prison will reduce crime; that financial targets drive performance or that people will follow rules – even when the evidence suggests otherwise. Unfortunately, the simple lie or a willingness to put our faith in the illusion of control looks even more attractive during times of crisis. We find comfort in certainty and rational, empirical thinking at the best of times, but this trait is intensified when we feel threatened. It is why electorates invariably shift to the right during times of political or economic upheaval. In his book *The Audacity of Hope*, Barack Obama describes the appeal of Ronald Reagan's homespun, simplistic message in the aftermath of the late 1970s recession and the Iran hostage crisis: 'I understood his appeal. It was the same appeal as the military bases back in Hawaii had always held for me as a young boy, with their tidy streets and well-oiled machinery,

---

[31] Edward de Bono blog, 18 August 2006, www.debonoblog.com

the crisp uniforms and crisper salutes. Reagan spoke to America's longing for order, our need to believe that we are not simply subject to blind, impersonal forces but that we can shape our individual and collective destinies.'[32]

Just like electorates during times of political or financial instability, the instinct of many business leaders to retrench in the wake of the recent economic turmoil is understandable. When you are under attack, when allies seem thin on the ground, human nature tells you to keep your head down. Try to marshal the chaos into something that can be controlled. Loosening up during a crisis seems counter-intuitive. Distrust everyone: employees, customers and other stakeholders, they are all out to get you. Don't even trust yourself to make the right decisions, but only act when you have complete certainty about the likely outcome and abide by the narrow mantra of 'If you can't measure it, don't do it'.[33] At the same time, adopt a tight, hierarchical approach to all communication, banning anything that hasn't been through the most rigorous approval processes and legal checks. Experimentation is risk and risk is inherently a bad thing.

James Boyle, the author of *Public Domain*, describes this mindset as 'cultural agoraphobia', which 'leads us always to emphasize the downsides of openness and lack of central control and to overvalue the virtues of order and authority'.[34]

---

[32] Barack Obama, *The Audacity of Hope: Thoughts on reclaiming the American dream*, Canongate Books, 2008.

[33] This is a corruption of the quote usually attributed to Peter Drucker, 'If you can't measure it, you can't manage it.' I have heard it used on numerous occasions to justify why a particular programme or project, that happens to be difficult to measure, is too risky to pursue.

[34] James Boyle, *Public Domain: Enclosing the commons of the mind*, Yale University Press, 2009.

Boyle focuses on two simple stories to illustrate his point. Minitel was an early version of the internet: a highly reliable and authoritative online information source, controlled by the French government via the state-owned France Telecom. Compared to Minitel, the World Wide Web is a chaotic and uncontrollable environment, full of propaganda and pornography, in which no one is in overall control, quality is variable in the extreme and anyone can publish whatever they want. Boyle also invites us to compare the *Encyclopaedia Britannica* – a wonderfully authoritative source of information, produced by a team of eminent academics and lexicographers – with Wikipedia, put together by a loosely co-ordinated group of enthusiastic amateurs. In both cases, and without the benefit of hindsight, which option would we have chosen? The truth is that the vast majority of us, driven by a fear of chaos and a love of order (Boyle's 'cultural agoraphobia'), would have been instinctively drawn to the tighter, more controllable and seemingly more authoritative Minitel and *Encylopaedia Britannica*.

Boyle was writing from the perspective of an intellectual property law expert and striving to find a balance between the protection of rights holders and the public good. His thesis is not that of a typical libertarian, arguing for complete deregulation or unrestricted access to all creative content. He simply suggests that given a choice between (what I would describe as) loose and tight, our instincts are invariably wrong: 'It is not that openness is always right. It is not. Often we need strong intellectual property rights, privacy controls, and networks that demand authentication. Rather, it is that we need a balance between open and closed, owned and free, and we are systematically likely to get the balance wrong.'

THE HIGH PRICE OF CONTROL

Not only does tight not work, but the control illusion that underpins it – an illusion propagated by legions of consultants, economists, market researchers and other purveyors of empirical snake oil – has actually made businesses less capable of embracing the complex realities of the modern world. After decades of investing huge amounts of money on consultants and hiring expensive forecasters, planners, analysts, econometricians, compliance officers and an army of spreadsheet-wielding MBAs, are the decisions made by our corporations any more effective? Are our leaders any smarter than those who have gone before or are our institutions better equipped to handle what the world throws their way? All too often, to use a sporting metaphor, it is like sportsmen spending so long pumping iron in the gym that they end up too muscle-bound to actually perform on the pitch.

The people at the top of the leading management consultancies would naturally argue in favour of the merits of taking a more analytical or empirical approach. According to Ian Davis, worldwide managing director of McKinsey: 'Long-gone is the day of the gut-instinct management style. Today's business leaders are adopting algorithmic decision-making techniques and using highly sophisticated software to run their organizations.'[35] Professor Roger Martin, Dean of the Rotman School of Management at the University of Toronto, describes himself as 'a recovering strategy consultant' – a tongue-in-cheek homage to his days with the Monitor global strategy consultancy. It is hardly surprising that Martin sees things differently from

---

[35] *McKinsey Quarterly*, January 2006.

the people at McKinsey: 'Let me suggest an alternative trend – the rise of heuristics [the application of intuition or common sense to problem solving] over algorithms; qualitative over quantitative research; judgement over analytics, creativity over crunching. Smart executives are recognizing that the analytic approach to business has overreached.'[36] Recent developments, such as the emergence of behavioural economics and the use of more creative approaches to market research, would suggest that the tide is turning in favour of Martin's view of the world. There will always be a place for sound analysis, the application of sophisticated data and clever software, but not at the expense of judgement, intuition and creativity.

The vast amount of time and energy that businesses spend on compliance, forecasting, market research, data crunching, strategic planning and strategic risk assessments has also added a huge cost and administrative burden. The recently established Independent Parliamentary Standards Authority (IPSA), created in the wake of the MPs' expenses scandal, provides a perfect illustration of the high cost of compliance. Created at a cost of £6.6 million – which, incidentally, is six times the amount that the errant MPs were forced to repay – the IPSA is rumoured to require an annual budget of £6 million and 80 staff to manage MPs' expense claims. Not only is it expensive, but the system it operates has been widely criticized for being slow, ridiculously bureaucratic (even small items, such as office stationery, have to be claimed for) and unnecessarily complicated. That said, any sympathy the media and public may have had for those suffering at the hands of the bureaucrats was soon quashed when IPSA provided the

---

[36] Quoted in *Marketing* magazine 20 May 2009.

press with accounts of its staff being verbally abused by a handful of frustrated MPs.

We might accept that an expensive and overly bureaucratic compliance system is a small price to pay to protect the integrity of our parliamentary democracy, but away from Westminster, imagine how much is invested by businesses and other institutions on unwieldy compliance functions, risk assessments that fail to anticipate future problems, strategic reports and detailed job descriptions that will never be read, detailed pieces of data analysis that don't reach any conclusions, market research that fails to generate any insights, grand strategic plans that can't be implemented. Selling the illusion of tight is an expensive business.

THE SEARCH FOR NEW THINKING

This book isn't written from the perspective of Silicon Valley or some other hotbed of new age and often, to a northern European ear, somewhat naive business thinking. It is hopefully grounded in real business – what I typically describe, somewhat unfairly, as 'the world of big, boring companies, dealing with everyday big, boring issues'. I have therefore included as many case studies on major corporations as I have on the type of smaller, leading-edge enterprises that tend to dominate most business books. During the first part of this book I will explore the forces that underpin the need to loosen up, from the increasing complexity facing all institutions and the growth of new types of informal collective behaviour to the impact of social media and generational shifts at the top and bottom of the corporate hierarchy. I will then describe what I would characterize as the end of certainty – a collapse of faith in the tight, empirical, rational models that underpinned our financial and political systems and approach to business – and how this is being replaced by a new wave of thinking in many of our financial institutions, corporations, business schools and political parties. The launch of David Cameron's Big Society vision and the new coalition government's use of participative techniques to involve the electorate in policy and spending decisions, have provided me with a particularly timely case study on what appears to be a loosening of the political process. There is talk in the corridors of Westminster about the emergence of a 'post-bureaucratic age', brought about by the transformational power of the internet and the public's desire to scrutinize the behaviour of its so-called political masters. This trend appears to be mirrored on the other side of the Atlantic, with the emergence of the Tea Party movement, a grassroots political force without any clear leadership, definable structure or coherent agenda, other than a visceral hatred of government in general and Barack Obama's policies in particular.

I am also trying to make a balanced argument. Business theories, models and definitions of what constitutes good business practice are innately oppositional. Every iconoclastic, sweeping assertion by the evangelists of social media and Silicon Valley thinking, criticizing generally accepted business practices, receives a counterblast from business professionals, who regard much of this thinking as puerile, contrarian and naïve nonsense. Finding a pragmatic balance, without appearing to sit on the fence, is tricky. It is always easier to write a polemical rant than a sober assessment of pros and cons, but I believe that the necessary oversimplification at the heart of any polemical argument makes it difficult to apply any lessons to the real world. Clever soundbites and glib management aphorisms rarely translate into smart strategies. My contention therefore is that institutions cannot be entirely loose – there has to be some structure and organizing principle, otherwise complete chaos will ensue. In the words of Kai Peters, chief executive of Ashridge Business School, 'Bureaucracy is slow and cumbersome, but generally cost effective and reliable. Absolute decentralisation is creative and exciting, but it leads to duplication, generates a myriad of micro-systems and is ultimately frustrating and expensive.'[37] But by the same token, an excessive reverence for tight ways of thinking and working is delusional, expensively counter-productive and fails to bring the best out of people. There has to be freedom, but within a framework.

Paradoxically, for any institution, being loose is far more difficult than being tight. It takes time and effort to create an organizational culture that can operate without a command and control mindset. Business guru Peter Drucker talked about how 'flexible free-form organizations place greater load on their members than do the traditional command and control structures',[38] while Abraham Maslow made the point that a more democratic style of management was more demanding than an authoritarian approach, because it required more of the individual. It is all too easy to see why lazy leaders and weak institutions revert to authoritarianism and the illusion of control; it just saves time.

---

[37] *Management Today*, March 2010.
[38] Quoted in Carol Kennedy, *Guide to Management Gurus*, Random House Business, 2007.

FIGHTING THE SOCIAL NORM

There are also some powerful social barriers to loose think-ing. Readers of the *Daily Mail* may bemoan the emergence of a permissive society, reflecting the liberal and what they would regard as irresponsible values of the 1960s, but the reality is that society has become increasingly tight. New laws, new forms of surveillance and a huge compliance infra-structure – from traffic wardens and surveillance camera operators to health and safety officers – have been put in place to control our behaviour. And broadly speaking, the vast majority of us like it this way, so much so that society tends to turn on people prepared to go against the norm.

Oliver and Gillian Schonrock are unlikely heroes, but they can be legitimately labelled as champions of a loose way of thinking. The couple found themselves in the middle of a media storm during the summer of 2010, when news leaked out that their local education authority had threat-ened to report them to social services. Their crime? Allowing their children aged eight and five to cycle the one mile from their home in Dulwich, South London to school and back. The Schonrocks argued that they felt it important for their children to enjoy the same level of freedom from parental supervision that they themselves had enjoyed as children. Battle lines were quickly drawn between commentators and members of the public who admired the couple's laid-back attitude and others who felt their actions were completely irresponsible. Boris Johnson, the arch libertarian Mayor of London, was predict-ably on the side of the Schonrocks. Writing in the *Daily Telegraph* he said, 'Instead of hounding the Schonrocks we should start doing everything we can to make their dream come true.'[39] He followed this with a typical piece of Johnsonian rhetoric in support of them: 'They have taken the sword of commonsense to the great bloated encephalopathic[40] sacred cow of "elf" and safety and of course are being persecuted by the authorities.'[41] He has recently backed-up the rhetoric by trying to persuade the authorities in London to allow children to cycle on the pavements.

The Schonrocks might find inspiration in a website created by another parent, whose loose approach to childcare put her at odds with conventional thinking. Lenore Skenazy is a mother with a mission. In the spring of 2008 she allowed her nine-year-old son to travel unaccompanied on the New York subway, from Bloomingdale's, in the middle of Manhattan, to the family home. She then wrote about it in her column for the *New York Sun*. As was the case with the Schronrocks, Skenazy's action catalysed a heated debate about the amount of freedom that parents should give their children. She argued that New York is now one of the safest cities in America and that when her son made it home and without mishap, he was 'fairly levitating with pride'. When confronted by the inevitable media storm, she tried to put things in perspective: 'My son had not climbed Mt Fuji in flip-flops. He did not decode his own DNA. He'd simply done what most people of my age had done routinely when they were his age: gone somewhere on his own, without a security detail.'[42] The media controversy encouraged Skenazy to create her Free Range Kids blog, to

---

[39] *Daily Telegraph*, 5 July 2010.
[40] I had to look this up as well. It is a disease of the brain. Boris was clearly paying attention during O-level biology.
[41] Quoted in the *Observer*, 11 July 2010.
[42] Interview in *The Times*, 9 June 2008.

provide a platform for her belief that parents should stop being so paranoid about the safety of their children.

When it comes to the protection of our children, tight thinking has become the social norm. We live in a risk-averse, litigious culture, we are obsessed with health and safety and feel irresponsible if we don't keep our children under supervision at all times. Even the health and safety experts, who are invariably blamed for over-reacting, have called for a greater balance between risks and benefits when it comes to bringing up our children. The chief executive of the Royal Society for the Prevention of Accidents has suggested that, 'We need to accept that uncertainty is inherent in adventure and this contains the possibility of adverse outcomes. A young person's development should not be unduly stifled by the proper need to consider the worst consequences of risk but must be balanced by its likelihood and indeed its benefits.'[43] The new Education Secretary, Michael Gove, has joined the chorus in favour of fewer restrictions, calling for 'a *Dangerous Book for Boys* culture'[44] and criticizing the 'bubble-wrapped culture' that he believes is the norm in UK schools.

But at the moment, society emphasizes the risks and appears to demand that children are raised in virtual captivity and not allowed to make decisions for themselves. One of the simplest manifestations of parental tight thinking has been the dramatic increase in the number of children who are now driven to school, rather than walk or use public transport: the number of seven- to eight-year-olds who walk to school on their own in the UK has declined from 80 per cent in 1971 to

[43] Quoted in *The Times*, 2 July 2010.
[44] Quoted in the *Sunday Times*, 12 September 2010. He references Conn and Hal Iggulden's *The Dangerous Book for Boys*, HarperCollins, 2006.

only 10 per cent in 2010.[45] The sad irony is that the biggest risk to those children who actually walk to school is from the large number of cars charging up to the school gates. As the Schonrocks and Skenazy discovered, challenging the tight thinking that underpins the approach of most of our institutions – no matter how spurious the rational and empirical logic they use to bolster their arguments – is rarely easy.

For twenty-five years the Seattle-based retailer, Nordstrom, operated its business using an employee manual that consisted of a small card handed out to each new employee. On the front it read: 'Welcome to Nordstrom. We're glad to have you with our company. Our number one goal is to provide outstanding customer service. Set both your personal and professional goals high. We have great confidence in your ability to achieve them. So our employee handbook is very simple. We only have one rule'. On the back of the card it read: 'Our only rule: Use good judgement in all situations." The only supplementary advice provided was to, 'Please feel free to ask your department manager, store manager, or division general manager any question at any time.'[46] Unfortunately, this simple piece of advice and very public demonstration of trust in its employees, that served the company well for so many years, has become something of a museum piece. The welcome pack for new Nordstrom employees continues to include the card, but also features a more conventional handbook of rules and regulations highlighting how even the most enlightened businesses were helpless in the face of the rising tide of litigation and

---

[45] Statistic quoted in *The Times*, 15 September 2010.
[46] *The Nordstrom Way to Customer Service Excellence: A handbook for implementing great service in your organization*, Robert Spector and Patrick McCarthy, John Wiley & Sons, 2005.

compliance. The irony is that the Nordstrom manual story has been rediscovered by the social media generation, who hold it up as a perfect example of the type of trusting corporate behaviour that is necessary when dealing with employees' use of social media. Meg Pickard, writing in the *Guardian* about the media owner's new social media guidelines for staff, was one of many to reference the Nordstrom story. In her view: 'An exhaustive list of commandments is rarely the best way to influence behaviour. Prescriptive rules have the effect of infantilising staff, and make it harder for them to adapt to different situations. This goes as much for digital communication as for selling socks ... Like the Nordstrom handbook, we're trusting staff to follow the spirit, not just the letter, of our guidelines.'[47] It is time to rediscover the original spirit of the Nordstrom manual and challenge the assumption that people cannot be trusted, that rules and regulations are the only way to control our behaviour and that the only alternative to tight complicance is organizational chaos.

---

[47] *Guardian*, 1 November 2010.

CHAPTER 2

A TIGHT WORLD BEGINS TO UNRAVEL

A POTENT COMBINATION OF cultural, technological and economic trends is forcing institutions to abandon the tight ways of thinking and working, that they have hitherto relied on, and embrace the need to loosen up. The focus of the first part of this book will be on the interplay of these trends and how different institutions are responding to them. I will begin with an analysis of the increasing levels of complexity facing all institutions, from the need to accommodate new patterns of consumer behaviour and changing expectations, to the explosive growth in the amount of (often contradictory) data filling the in-trays of the world's business and political leaders. This is being accompanied by the emergence of new forms of collective behaviour, which both demonstrate the new power of loose, informal networks, and also underline the deficiencies of the tight, bureaucratic structures that have to deal with them. Crowds can become forces for good or mobs hell-bent on undermining traditional sources of authority; they can be wise or irrational, creative or highly destructive. Dealing with them forces institutions to loosen up, whether they are simply trying to cope with the speed at which popular movements are formed or attempting to harness the spirit of collective creativity that they unleash.

Another cultural change encouraging looser ways of thinking and working is the generational shift that is happening at the top and bottom of the corporate hierarchy. Although it is dangerous to generalize about the shared attitudes and behaviours of a particular generation, there are signs of a less formal, more collaborative, post baby-boomer mindset beginning to take hold at the top of our businesses and political parties. There is also plenty of evidence that the outlook and behaviour of the generation beginning to enter the workforce – the first group to have truly grown up in the digitally interactive world – have very different expectations of the workplace and require a fundamentally different approach from their managers.

While this isn't specifically a book about social media, its impact provides a thread throughout much of my narrative. I prefer to emphasize the socio-cultural and behavioural aspects of the social media revolution, rather than simply the technological. My argument is that these behaviours are powered by technology, not necessarily created by them, although it is a circular argument: what comes first, the technology or the behavioural and attitudinal change? The point is that to see the rise of social media as purely a technological trend risks missing the bigger picture. One of the best ways I have found to describe the challenge posed by new patterns of consumer behaviour and changing expectations is that the connected consumer is now coming face-to-face with the disconnected corporation. I will explore why many institutions struggle to live by the simple principles that define success in this new world and also how social media has the potential to become a highly powerful change agent, dramatizing the structural, operational and philosophical weaknesses of most organizations.

2.1 NOT A PLACE FOR TIDY MINDS

'We are seeing a large number of mixed signals in both the market and our customers' expectations, and we think the words "unusual uncertainty" are an accurate description of what is occurring.'

John Chambers, chief executive, Oracle[48]

During the opening weeks of his new musical *Love Never Dies*, the long-awaited (for some) sequel to *Phantom of the Opera*, Sir Andrew Lloyd-Webber expressed much frustration about the damage caused to advance ticket sales by the comments and reviews of amateur critics on the internet. There is an accepted principle in theatre-land that the professional critics don't formally review a performance until all of the teething problems have been ironed out. Unfortunately, the amateur critics refuse to follow this convention, so reviews of *Love Never Dies* began to appear within hours of the opening performance. The professional critics joined the debate in an attempt to defend the primacy of their viewpoint, compared with the uninformed opinions of bloggers, although their argument was somewhat undermined when it was discovered that a pun repeated by a number of eminent critics – 'Paint never dries' – actually originated from one of the amateur commentators. Veteran critic Michael Coveney spoke for many in his profession when he suggested that, 'Everyone is entitled to their opinion but it is not criticism.'[49] In his *Guardian* theatre blog, David Cote made a typically valiant defence of his profession, even if the metaphor he used was rather untheatrical: 'We

---

[48] Comment during a call with analysts, 12 August 2010.
[49] *Observer*, 14 March 2010.

critics, reviewers, consumer reporters – call us what you will – are the dung beetles of culture. We consume excrement, enriching the soil and protecting livestock from bacterial infection in the process. We are intrinsic to the theatre ecology. Eliminate us at your peril.'[50]

There is little doubt that the dung beetles are fighting a losing battle against this type of evolutionary process. This view was endorsed by Andrew Keen, author of *The Cult of the Amateur*: 'There is a general rebellion against the cultural critic and against the notion that somebody else can tell someone what they should watch or read. The web is a platform for that rebellion, but it is also the cause of it. There is something in online culture that lends itself to rebellion.'[51] It is a rebellion that appears to be taking hold. *Variety* magazine in the US has already dispensed with its chief film and theatre critics. The days of the professional critic appear numbered. The EdTwinge project is typical of the type of grassroots, amateur initiative, enabled by social media, that is beginning to threaten the hegemony of the professional critics. Created by an Edinburgh-based team of digital creatives and PR people in their spare time, EdTwinge is a website, built around a sophisticated algorithm, which aggregates the tweeted comments and reviews of the thousands of people who attend the Edinburgh Festival every August. By tapping into the collective wisdom of the festival crowd and leveraging smart, low-cost technology, EdTwinge provides a dynamic, real-time summary of the views of real people.

The rise of the amateur has even permeated the rarefied,

---

[50] *Guardian* theatre blog, 10 March 2010.
[51] *Guardian*, 14 March 2010.

elitist world of fashion. The front row in any fashion show has always been the place where you will find the editors of the leading fashion magazines, rubbing shoulder pads with assorted celebrities. Now the fashion houses have started offering these prized places to influential bloggers, even providing them with small desks for their computers. Many of the traditional fashion journalists have been relegated to the anonymity of the third row of the top shows, much to their disgust. The London *Evening Standard* described how one famous fashion journalist, being transported between fashion shows in a courtesy car, wound down his window to shriek, 'Help! Get me out! I'm with the bloggers!'[52]

A couple of years ago when I co-wrote *Crowd Surfing*[53] with David Brain, we depicted a world in which the empowered consumer was threatening the primacy of all traditional forms of authority and expertise, from politicians to GPs, CEOs to Church leaders. One of our key conclusions was that those businesses and leaders genuinely thriving in the chaos and complexity of the modern world weren't necessarily the most technologically accomplished, well resourced or working in what could be characterized as leading-edge businesses. They were simply more comfortable with the mess and uncertainty that surrounded them. They were happy to accept ambiguity and appeared to adopt a much looser approach to the way that they ran their businesses or political parties, whether delegating authority to their employees, sharing previously proprietary information with people outside their businesses or collaborating with customers. This philosophy was best expressed by

---

[52] *Evening Standard*, 8 July 2010.
[53] Martin Thomas & David Brain, *Crowd Surfing: Surviving and thriving in the age of consumer empowerment*, A&C Black, 2008.

Procter & Gamble's former chairman and CEO, A. G. Lafley, who talked about how businesses 'are operating in what is very much a "let go" world',[54] and by WPP's Sir Martin Sorrell, who commented that 'the 21st century is not for tidy minds'.[55]

The world has certainly not got any tidier in the few years since Sorrell made this remark. The failure of the global financial system, economic recession, environmental threats and continued political instability in the Middle East and Asia have made life even more confusing and complicated. New technology – and particularly the pace of change in the online world, typified by innovations such as the emergence of social media and mobile computing – has compounded this sense of confusion. We appear to be living through what Harvard economist Joseph Schumpeter described as a period of 'creative destruction': one of those dramatic phases of techno-logical innovation and new thinking that periodically refreshes the capitalist system. Our world is messy and bewilderingly complex and the public mood is cynical, mildly subversive and increasingly adversarial. It is a situation that defies rational analysis and neat, simple solutions, no matter how superficially attractive they might appear. It places a premium on speed and the ability to improvise over cautious deliberation and longer-term planning.

---

[54] Speaking at the Association of National Advertisers conference, 10 July 2006.
[55] Quoted in *Management Today*, April 2008.

A WORLD OF COMPLEXITY

A global study by IBM in 2009 revealed that 79 per cent of CEOs expected complexity to increase, while only 49 per cent felt prepared for it.[56] In his foreword to the study, Samuel J. Palmisano, chairman, president and CEO of IBM Corporation talks about how, 'events, threats and opportunities aren't just coming at us faster or with less predictability; they are converging and influencing each other to create entirely unique situations.' It is the uniqueness of these situations that is the key point, creating a whole new set of challenges for our business and political leaders, for which their training, MBAs and experience have left them largely ill-prepared. Apart from macro-economic factors, the study showed that a key driver of this perceived complexity was the explosion in the amount of structured and unstructured data, generated by new technology, that is now available for the CEOs and their teams to try to make sense of. It quoted Julian Segal, managing director and CEO, Caltex Australia Limited, saying that, 'The world is non-linear, so the ability to cut through complexity relies on processing a large amount of information quickly and extracting nuggets to make quick decisions. Building advantage will be an outcome of dealing with complexity better than our competitors.' We all appear to be faced with our own version of Moore's Law,[57] in which the amount of data we have to

---

[56] 'Capitalising on Complexity, Insights from the Global Chief Executive Officer Study', IBM, 2009.

[57] The original Moore's Law, coined by Intel's founder Gordon E. Moore, predicted that the number of transistors that can be placed inexpensively on an integrated circuit doubles every two years. Other definitions have the figure doubling every 18 months, although two years appears to be the most widely accepted definition.

process, from emails to social media updates, doubles every two years, but without a similar rate of improvement in our cognitive abilities.

This feeling of being overwhelmed by complexity appears to be shared by the general public. A study by Bristol University, published during the summer of 2010, claimed that Britain is a 'nation consumed by too much choice'.[58] According to the report, agonizing about choices keeps 42 per cent of people awake at night, while 47 per cent of us find that even small decisions are hard to make. The report's author, Harriet Bradley, professor of sociology at Bristol University, summarized the public's mood by suggesting that, 'We seem to live in a wonderful world of options, but it can actually be quite frightening and scary.'[59] She blamed the 'constant stream of new media, daily technological advancements and aggressive multimedia advertising' for turning us into 'a nation of indeciders'.[60] The report echoed many of the themes in Barry Schwartz's book *The Paradox of Choice*, in which he argued that, 'As the number of choices we face increases, freedom of choice eventually becomes a tyranny of choice.'[61]

The 2008 US presidential campaign provided us with a perfect illustration of the challenges faced by organizations when trying to cut through the information clutter. Writing in the *New York Times*, Adam Nagourney described how the candidates struggled to break through: 'the day's crush of blog

---

[58] 'Confused Nation' report, Department of Sociology, University of Bristol, 2010.
[59] Quoted in *The Times*, 3 August 2010.
[60] http://www.bristol.ac.uk/news, 3 August 2010.
[61] Barry Schwartz, *The Paradox of Choice, Why more is less*, HarperCollins, 2005.

postings, cable television headlines, television advertisements, speeches by other candidates and surrogates, video press releases, screaming emailed charges and counter-charges – not to mention the old-fashioned newspaper article or broadcast report on the evening news.'[62] He quoted one political expert saying that, 'the ability to drive a message narrative is all but impossible.' It is a sentiment shared by many communications professionals beyond the world of politics, who are trying to engage increasingly disengaged and distracted audiences.

John Naughton, professor of the public understanding of technology at the Open University, is one of the smartest thinkers on the impact of the internet on the way society thinks and works. He has described how the communications technology revolution has created a situation in which 'Complexity is the new reality', but a reality that most institutions have struggled to come to terms with: 'Traditionally, organisations have tried to deal with the problem by reducing complexity – acquiring competitors, locking in customers, producing standardised products and services, etc. These strategies are unlikely to work in our emerging environment, where intelligence, agility, responsiveness and a willingness to experiment (and fail) provide better strategies for dealing with what the networked world will throw at you.'[63] We may aspire to simplicity, but, as discussed earlier, whether trying to understand the impact of new technology, international politics, macro-economic theory or human behaviour, oversimplification is rarely the answer.

---

[62] *New York Times*, 15 September 2008.
[63] 'Everything you ever wanted to know about the Internet', *Observer*, 20 June 2010.

HOLDING INSTITUTIONS TO ACCOUNT

There is also a new economic and commercial reality, which is characterized by intense market competition, a more circumspect and thrifty consumer and the unrelenting scrutiny of shareholders, stakeholders, activists, employees and legislators. People expect to be able to hold institutions to account, whether they work for them, buy their products, live in their neighbourhoods or are affected by their actions. They have been aided by people like Marcus Williamson, the man behind the www.ceoemail.com website, which provides the personal email addresses of Britain's leading bosses, allowing customers to bypass the normal complaints process. According to Williamson, 'A complaint via the CEO's office was handled better and more promptly than one going through normal channels',[64] which, if nothing else, is an indictment of the inefficiency of most customer complaints departments.

Businesses guilty of what the public decides is irresponsible behaviour will be taken to task within hours. So when the Primark retail chain started selling padded bikini tops for girls as young as seven, a combination of the Mumsnet social media forum and the Children's Society forced it into a rapid retreat. Bras also became a hot topic for M&S. A wonderfully named web-based protest group called Busts for Justice forced the retailer to stop charging well-endowed customers more for larger bra sizes. The story featured all of the usual consumer empowerment traits – angry individual decides to air grievances on Facebook, attracts sympathetic supporters (almost 17,000 at the last count, including a fair number of men), generates

---

[64] Quoted in *The Times*, 14 September 2010.

mainstream media headlines and ultimately forces the company into an embarrassing climbdown. Similarly, cosmetics brand MAC was forced to rebrand a collection inspired by the Mexican town of Ciudad Juárez, when a group of fashion bloggers pointed out the inappropriateness of linking a beauty brand to a town infamous for the number of murders of females.

These are all instances in which the companies deserved public censure, but there have been other occasions when the merits of holding institutions to account have been far less clear cut. During 2010, the US intelligence services were faced with a serious challenge when more than 90,000 intelligence documents, relating to the war in Afghanistan, were leaked by the WikiLeaks website. It was feared that the lives of both CIA operatives and local informants would be put at risk by the revelations and it created a heated media debate about the rights and wrongs of disclosing sensitive documents and the definition of 'the public interest'. WikiLeaks describes itself as a 'multi-jurisdictional public service designed to protect whistleblowers, journalists and activists who have sensitive materials to communicate to the public' and argues that 'transparency in government activities leads to reduced corruption, better government and stronger democracies'.[65] It was established in Sweden in 2006 by a group of human rights activists, technology experts and journalists and takes its inspiration from one of the most notorious leaks of all time: when in 1971 top secret papers about America's political and military involvement in Vietnam were published in the *New York Times*. It provides an outlet for whistleblowers, journalists

---

[65] http://wikileaks.org

and anyone else who believes they are in possession of sensitive information that is in the public interest, but which, primarily for legal reasons, cannot be published through normal media channels. One of the founders of WikiLeaks, Julian Assange, a former computer hacker,[66] became the focus of the huge amount of public and media criticism of the decision to leak the intelligence documents: *The Times* described it as 'a potential death list' and argued that, 'These leaks may be a triumph for citizen journalism . . . but in the wrong hands they are also an execution warrant.'[67] Unabashed, Assange continued to argue that WikiLeaks was occupying the moral high ground and standing up for the fundamental principles of good journalism: 'We are creating a space behind us that permits a form of journalism which lives up to the name that journalism has always tried to establish for itself.'[68]

WikiLeaks is typical of a new type of activist movement, armed with a sophisticated understanding of new technology, an army of enthusiastic volunteers and the skills to force even the largest corporations to respond to their agenda. It has no permanent office, no salaried staff and is funded purely through donations. Organizations such as WikiLeaks are also aided by the fact that the distribution of power in the online world is asymmetric. All of the advantages now lie with the activists. They have the expertise to use the latest technology – the WikiLeaks team uses cryptography to hide the identity of its people and make it next to impossible to trace content to a specific internet address – and know how to get the online

---

[66] He co-authored (with Suelette Dreyfus) *Underground: Tales of hacking, madness and obsession on the electronic frontier*, Reed Books Australia, 1997.

[67] *The Times*, Leader, 29 July 2010.

[68] Quoted in the *Observer*, 1 August 2010.

community on their side by playing the freedom-of-expression card. They can invariably rely on a corporate over-reaction – usually involving lawyers trying to sue or silence online critics – to keep the blogosphere in a state of mild hysteria. They can also rely on the power of anonymity, with critics of corporate behaviour able to masquerade under a variety of pseudonyms. The journalist Quentin Letts included 'webnonymous' in his list of the *50 People Who Buggered Up Britain* and described how it was 'wrecking the tone of public discussion. It is lowering it to the grottiest level of invective and allows interested parties to present an unbalanced view of public opinion'.[69] In an interesting response to this asymmetry, the *Sun Chronicle* in Massachusetts has started charging people to leave comments on its website. The amount involved is minimal – a one-off charge of only 99 cents – but by insisting that it is paid by credit card, the media owner can ensure that a real person's name appears against every comment. This has, not surprisingly, unleashed a fierce debate about whether this insistence on people using their real names undermines their right to free speech, but if it proves to be successful, it has the potential to reduce the amount of offensive commentary that often makes it difficult to have a balanced and reasonable debate on many social media platforms.

DISTRUST AND SUBVERSION

Much of the success of activist movements and the growing public desire to scrutinize or question the behaviour and motives

---

[69] Quentin Letts, *50 People Who Buggered Up Britain*, Constable, 2009.

of organizations is motivated by a lack of trust. People's faith in all forms of institution has collapsed, not least a political system in the UK undermined by the long-running MPs' expenses scandal. The Edelman Trustbarometer[70] is widely regarded as the most authoritative study of the way that 'informed publics' – essentially college-educated, media-savvy and reasonably affluent individuals in the world's largest economies – view the world's business and political leaders and the institutions that they run. The 2010 study revealed that although trust in business had recovered slightly from the traumas of 2009 – when the figure plummeted to an all-time low – business, government and the media all continue to experience a significant trust deficit. In the UK, 49 per cent of people claimed that they trusted business to do what is right, which represented a modest improvement on the 46 per cent figure reported in 2009, whereas trust in government, during the final months of the Brown administration, had slipped from 40 to 38 per cent. The only sector to fare worse was, of course, the banks, with trust levels slipping to 21 per cent, compared to 41 per cent in the pre-recession days of 2007. The findings in the other developed, Western markets were broadly similar, with fewer than half the population trusting business, government or the media. Cynicism remains the default setting, with 70 per cent of respondents saying that institutions will revert to old financial habits when the economic crisis is over. Their cynicism is probably justified, given the rapid return of the high bonus culture in the City, despite a climate of austerity in the wider economy.

This public shows its disenchantment with institutions and

---

[70] http://www.edelman.co.uk/trustbarometer

distrust for authority by displaying a subversive streak. The battle for the number one slot in the UK pop charts at Christmas isn't quite as important as it used to be, but it still has a symbolic significance for artists and record labels. For the last few years it has almost been guaranteed that the Christmas number one is provided by the winning artist from Simon Cowell's *X Factor* television show. Things had become so predictable – after four successive Christmas number ones from *X Factor* artists – that the bookies had even stopped taking bets on which artist would top the charts during Christmas 2009: it was bound to be the latest *X Factor* winner, Joe McElderry. This Cowell monopoly encouraged Jon Morter, a hi-fi technician and part-time DJ from Essex, and his wife, Tracey, to launch a Facebook group to promote the claims of a rival artist. They had tried something similar the previous year and although they had failed to beat the *X Factor* marketing machine, they had learnt how to work the system. They were motivated more by a sense of fun – describing their campaign as a 'silly idea' – rather than anger, but their choice of artist, Rage Against the Machine, was an obvious attack on the all-pervasive *X Factor* juggernaut. They launched their campaign with a straightforward appeal to the nation's subversive streak: 'Fed up of Simon Cowell's latest karaoke act being Christmas No 1? Me too . . . So who's up for a mass-purchase of the track 'KILLING IN THE NAME' . . . as a protest to the *X Factor* monotony?' Their Facebook group rapidly secured almost half a million members. Simon Cowell initially described the campaign as 'stupid' and 'cynical', but was smart enough to enter into the spirit of a competition that revived interest in the battle for the Christmas number one spot and boosted sales for his own artist. Ultimately, the nation's subversive streak won the day, with Rage Against the Machine's wonderfully unseasonal 'Killing in the Name' outselling McElderry by 50,000 copies. One music retailer described it as 'the greatest chart upset ever'.[71]

As well as symbolizing the subversive streak that doesn't lie too deep within the British psyche, the Rage Against the Machine campaign also demonstrated the ease with which largely informal popular movements are capable of competing with even the most sophisticated commercial marketing operations. Something similar happened during the 2010 Edinburgh Fringe, when an online poll to find the favourite comedy act during the Fringe over the past 30 years – created as a publicity gimmick by Foster's (which sponsors the annual Comedy Awards) – was hijacked by a subversively inclined public. The poll produced a highly unlikely winner in the shape of an obscure Japanese avant-garde musical comedy act, Frank Chickens. This particular protest campaign was triggered by the comedian and arch contrarian, Stewart Lee, who described the Foster's competition as the 'most shameful, inane thing I have seen in all the years I have been doing the Fringe'.[72] His main complaint was that this type of competition invariably favours recent, high-profile acts and mused that an obscure act from the 1980s, such as Frank Chickens, would have no chance of winning. His comments, shared in an email to a few friends, were picked up by other comedians, who then encouraged the thousands of their Twitter followers to follow Lee's recommendation.

The British public's subversive streak truly came to the fore during the 2010 general election campaign. It could be argued that this was the first election in which unofficial,

---

[71] BBC News, 20 December 2009.
[72] Stewart Lee's email to friends, subsequently leaked to the media.

informal and wonderfully subversive marketing became more of a factor than the official campaigns developed by the rival parties. Much of the advertising material produced during the election was fairly bland and unimaginative, so it may have been the case that the public were acting out of a sense of boredom when they started customizing the official campaigns. First blood went to the Labour Party activists who created a dedicated website – mydavidcameron.com – to provide a platform for people to produce their own versions of a Conservative poster featuring an obviously airbrushed photo of David Cameron and the message 'We can't go on like this'. It generated hundreds of spoof versions and people even began to customize the actual posters, in what Barbara Ellen in the *Observer* described as a case of 'the public channelling its "inner Banksy".'[73] My favourite spoof was produced by a creative soul in Hereford who gave Cameron an Elvis-style wig and changed the poster's message to 'We can't go on like this, with suspicious minds'.

The Conservative activists then entered into the subversive spirit of the occasion by producing their own spoof versions of a Labour Party campaign poster, which featured David Cameron in the guise of Gene Hunt, the lead character from BBC TV's *Ashes to Ashes* series and the message 'Don't let him take Britain back to the 1980s'. The creative idea for the original poster had been suggested by a Labour activist, rather than one of the party's official advertising agencies, which may explain why the Labour campaign team failed to anticipate how its message might backfire. The Gene Hunt character, brilliantly realized by Philip Glenister, may be a stereotype of a 1980s racist, chauvinist and bigoted police officer, but most

---

[73] *Observer*, 31 January 2010.

people find him strangely attractive. In one of the episodes, Hunt is described by his female sidekick as an 'overweight, over-the-hill, nicotine-stained, borderline alcoholic homophobe, with a superiority complex and an unhealthy obsession with male bonding'. To which he replies, 'You make that sound like a bad thing.'[74] As far as the British public is concerned, he certainly isn't a bad thing. Even Cameron said he was 'flattered' by Labour's comparison of him with Gene Hunt.[75]

George Osborne's press officer, Mesh Chhambra, appears to have been the first person to spot the opportunity, issuing a tweet that, 'Someone really should tell the PM to Fire Up the Quattro [one of the catchphrases from the show] . . . and get down the palace.' The Conservative Party campaign team quickly followed up Chhabra's suggestion, producing a new version of the poster, with a new slogan: 'Fire up the Quattro. It's time for change', accompanied by the line, 'Idea kindly donated by the Labour Party.' In a survey of Conservative Party activists after the election, conducted by the conservative home website, the home-made spoof was overwhelmingly voted as their favourite campaign poster. The official posters, expensively commissioned by the party's campaign team during the election, barely received a mention.

Subversively inclined electorates are not confined to the UK. The residents of Reykjavik have elected one of Iceland's top comedians, Jon Gnarr, to the post of mayor. His Best Party campaigned on a platform of clean politics, free towels in swimming pools and a new polar bear for the city's zoo. It also provided the electorate, which has been hit hard by the collapse of the Icelandic banks, with an opportunity to express

---

[74] BBC TV, *Ashes to Ashes*.
[75] BBC News, 3 April 2010.

its anger against the political and financial establishment. Gnarr was almost certainly the first male politican to show his commitment to a gay pride parade by turning up in drag, which is something that even Boris Johnson has yet to do – although I suspect it is a case of watch this space as far as London's mayor is concerned.

Subverting authority figures is one of the most obvious ways that the public is able to display its anger. I have a degree in history, so I am always a sucker for historical parallels. This probably explains why I was particularly taken by an article written by *The Times*' World Business Editor, Carl Mortished, in which he described the wave of consumer protest – against MPs, bankers and greedy business leaders acting against the interests of shareholders – as a 'peasants' revolt'. For those who drifted off during their history lessons, the original English Peasants' Revolt, led by Wat Tyler, occurred in 1381. When you study its causes, the parallels with today are all too obvious to Mortished: 'What irks voters, taxpayers and shareholders is what angered medieval peasants – that the ruling class regards us with contempt. It is the failure to acknowledge the duty owed, the failure of nobles to protect our interests.'[76] The same type of frustrations are being expressed by the members of the anti-Obama, Tea Party movement in the US, which argues that the political establishment in Washington is ignoring the needs and concerns of ordinary voters.

It isn't simply the Western democracies that are experiencing a 'peasants' revolt'. The Chinese government has traditionally shown little willingness to embrace the concept of consumer empowerment. The country's 160 million internet users have rarely risked using the internet to criticize party officials. In

---

[76] *The Times*, 28 May 2009.

fact, according to Evgeny Morozov, Yahoo fellow at Georgetown University, who has studied the way that authoritarian regimes have exploited the power of social media, the Chinese government can call on an army of 300,000 online supporters to 'game' the internet by flooding chat rooms with positive comments and links to pro-government sites. Nevertheless, in a landmark case in late 2008, a senior government official was dismissed for assaulting an 11-year-old girl, following a web-based protest. The incident, which occurred in a restaurant in Shenzhen, was captured on CCTV and rapidly spread around China's video-sharing websites. This created such a wave of online protest that even the Chinese government couldn't turn a blind eye.

During the following summer it appeared, for a brief period of time, that social media was about to deliver its first regime change. The disputed Iranian election, in which President Mahmoud Ahmadinejad was accused of rigging the vote against his reformist rival, Mir-Hossein Mousavi, created a storm of public protest. This intensified following the shooting of a protestor, Neda Soltani, which was captured by amateur photographers and rapidly circulated via social media. An electronic game of cat and mouse followed between the computer-literate dissidents – using social media to distribute photographs, videos and messages to the outside world – and government censors trying to shut down the technology and identify the ringleaders. The US State Department went so far as to persuade Twitter to postpone a planned shutdown of its service for a network upgrade, having recognized that it had become the activists' protest vehicle of choice. Lev Grossman, writing in *Time* magazine, described how, 'Twitter didn't start the protests in Iran, nor did it make them possible. But there's no question that it has emboldened the protesters, reinforced their conviction that they are not alone and engaged populations outside Iran in an emotional, immediate way that was never possible before.'[77] The digital commentator Clay Shirky described the events in Iran as 'the first revolution that has been catapulted onto a global stage and transformed by social media',[78] although, ultimately, a government crackdown on the use of the internet forced the protesters to revert to one of the oldest forms of social media (and a technique used during the Iranian Revolution in 1979) – shouting from rooftop to rooftop.

AMPLIFYING THE VOLUME OF MOANING

Procter & Gamble, the manufacturer of many of the world's leading consumer products, doesn't have to deal with many rooftop protests, but, like all major corporations, it has increasingly found itself at the mercy of critics, empowered by access to the internet and the belief that their views should be listened to. The company's global marketing officer Marc Pritchard has described the effect of social media as 'amplifying the volume of moaning'. He was speaking at the annual advertising festival in Cannes, in the wake of a social media-driven consumer protest about a new range of nappies, manufactured on behalf of P&G's Pampers brand. According to some parents, the nappies were giving their babies rashes, and following the template of all contemporary protest campaigns, they vented their anger through social media. More than 11,000 people joined a Facebook group demanding that

---

[77] *Time* magazine, 17 June 2009.
[78] Quoted in *The Times*, 21 June 2009.

P&G bring back the old style of Pampers. Pritchard, who is a vocal admirer of the power of social media, said that the company had actually received far more positive comments about the new Pampers range from people using traditional channels, such as helplines and letters, but that, 'The difference is Facebook had a much higher amplification of the negative comments. That is one of the things we have to deal with in the new world of brand building.'[79] Like all consumer-facing organizations, P&G has had to rethink the way that it handles customer feedback. There is little time for cautious deliberation: responses need to be almost immediate. And individual complaints can no longer be buried in the in-trays of the customer service department or within the confines of the call centre: they are now in the public domain and the corporate response is available for all to see.

It is one of the great ironies of consumer empowerment that it makes people less satisfied. As with all things in life, the more we have, the more we want. Which is why, despite the best efforts of our institutions (from government to commercial companies), customer satisfaction levels continue to decline. According to a study by Accenture and the Marketing Society,[80] the percentage of people whose 'expectations of service quality are frequently or always met' declined from 53 per cent in 2007 to 40 per cent in 2009. The depressing thought for any consumer-oriented business is that expectations will never be met and that satisfaction levels will always trend downwards. The rise of social media has clearly played a major part in accelerating this trend. Another Accenture study[81] revealed

---

[79] Quoted by FT.com, 24 June 2010.
[80] 'Start Making Sense', Accenture Global Consumer Satisfaction Report, 2009.
[81] Accenture 2009 Global Customer Satisfaction Study.

that not only do 89 per cent of consumers in the world's mature markets tell friends and colleagues about poor service, but 25 per cent now post reports online. The old adage in customer service departments used to be that a dissatisfied customer was likely to tell up to 10 friends about a poor product or service experience. That same customer, armed with a Facebook page or YouTube account, is now quite capable of telling 10 million.

Jim Murphy, editorial director at forecasting agency The Future Foundation, describes how we now live in a 'society of contestation'. His argument is that the collapse of trust in all forms of institutional power, and our willingness to challenge traditional sources of expertise and leadership, have created a situation in which customers can never be satisfied, electorates are almost ungovernable and employees virtually unmanageable. He describes how 'Authority has to battle for legitimacy every day; it can have no expectation of canned applause', and that, 'The truth as affirmed and broadcast by any institution is intrinsically, programmatically contestable. For every fact there is an anti-fact.'[82] Will Hutton makes a similar point when describing the highly partisan nature of broadcasting in the US, which unlike the UK, is not required to be impartial. This he argues is 'characteristic of a poisonous . . . public culture' because it completely undermines all attempts to have a balanced and reasoned debate on complex and often controversial policy issues. This has created a situation in which, 'Tough decisions – on banks, on fiscal policy, on defence, on the Middle East – have become almost impossible.'[83]

---

[82] 'Yes, No, Maybe, No, Yes: Corporate Life in the Contestation Nation', The Future Foundation (Spring 2010).
[83] Writing in the *Observer*, 25 July 2010.

The challenge of operating within a 'society of contestation' presents huge problems for all institutions, especially the scientific community. In his book *Denialism*,[84] the *New Yorker*'s science writer Michael Specter describes how the lack of faith in the scientific evidence produced by formerly trusted authorities is symptomatic of a society struggling to cope with 'the trauma of change'. No matter how much evidence is produced, the sceptics and refuseniks will always find a hole in any scientific argument that doesn't reflect their view of the world. G. K. Chesterton's aphorism 'When men stop believing in God, they don't believe in nothing. They believe in anything' should be reworked for the 21st century. Swap the word 'science' for 'God' and you have a pretty good sense of the prevailing view within a society in which the opinions of the people in the white lab coats are no longer trusted, whether defending the integrity of MMR vaccines, presenting the scientific evidence underpinning climate change or questioning the efficacy of homeopathy. This represents a huge challenge for the scientific community, which is increasingly losing the battle for hearts and minds, but it is also an issue for society as a whole – when we no longer trust the experts, who can we trust?

Even some of the empowerment evangelists have begun to question whether its effects are always benign. Ever since Shawn Fanning created the file-sharing software that led to the creation of Napster in 1999, there has been a contentious debate about the rights of creators and users of creative content in the digital age. There are strong arguments in favour of open technology platforms, which allow people to learn new skills and develop new applications. However, this point of view is

[84] Michael Specter, *Denialism: How irrational thinking hinders scientific progress, harms the planet, and threatens our lives*, Gerald Duckworth & Co, 2010.

countered by a growing backlash against the belief in the innate righteousness of those who advocate the idea of free access to creative content. Jaron Lanier is one of the original new media thinkers – he is credited with popularizing the term 'virtual reality'. In his book *You Are Not a Gadget*,[85] he criticizes the impact of what he terms 'hive thinking and "digital Maoism"' – open source software, the belief in the rights of free access to creative content – on individual creativity. This 'free content for all' philosophy represents the first time since the days of Robin Hood that the theft of other people's property, in the form of their creative content, has been allowed to assume the moral high ground. There is even a political party in Sweden, The Pirate Party, dedicated to promoting this belief. The party grew out of a protest movement which emerged when four founders of The Pirate Bay file-sharing site – which helped people share music tracks, TV and film content – were jailed and fined the equivalent of £2.4 million for what the Swedish court decided was a breach of copyright laws. The victory for The Pirate Party, which won a 7.1 per cent share of the popular vote in the 2009 European elections in Sweden, has provided a political platform for campaigners for file-sharing rights and the relaxation of copyright laws. A German Pirate Party also entered candidates in the European elections and a UK version took part in the 2010 general election under a platform of reforming copyright and patent law, ending excessive surveillance and promoting freedom of speech.

Lanier also takes issue with what reviewer John Tierney, in the *New York Times*, labels the 'vicious pack behaviour on blogs, forums and social networks – the meanness of mobs'.[86]

---

[85] Jaron Lanier, *You Are Not a Gadget: A Manifesto*, Allen Lane, 2010.
[86] *New York Times*, 11 January 2010.

We witnessed this phenomenon in the UK, in the aftermath of journalist Jan Moir's criticism of the gay lifestyle of Boyzone singer Stephen Gately. Around the same time as Moir was being roundly abused, broadcaster Andrew Neil found himself in trouble with the 'Twitterati' for an allegedly racist insult of his co-presenter Diane Abbott, when in an extended riff on people as biscuits, he described her as a chocolate hobnob; comedian Jimmy Carr was criticized for a typically close-to-the bone gag, linking troops wounded in Afghanistan to Britain's performance in future paralympic games; and writer A. A. Gill drew howls of protest when he wrote about how he had once killed a baboon. In each of these cases, in the words of the *Guardian*'s Jon Henley, 'a liberal rent a mob [were] hell bent on hanging out to dry those who express an opinion that differs from their own.'[87]

The author Eoin Colfer came up with his own technique for dealing with a social-media-based mob protest. He was confronted by a Facebook campaign, mounted by fans of *The Hitchhiker's Guide to the Galaxy*, who were outraged by his decision to write a sequel to the Douglas Adams novel. In an idle moment Colfer joined the Facebook group and being a contrarian, started posting critical messages about himself: 'Eoin Colfer is an a***hole', etc. Ironically, after reading these comments, the response of many of his former critics was to leap to his defence.

Colfer's tactic of adopting a policy of extreme self-criticism, in order to gain the sympathy vote, is one way of responding to the new public mood. For others in the public eye, it is more a case of being willing to embrace the chaos and ambiguity of modern life. Tom Peters talks about how, 'in an age when all

---

[87] *Guardian*, 31 October 2009.

value flows from creativity and initiative, we must imagine and embrace a model of leadership that is loose, open and perpetually imaginative.'[88] It is difficult to conceive of a looser leadership style than that embodied by Boris Johnson, the Mayor of London. His predecessor, Ken Livingstone, has described him as 'a lazy old fogie', without the self-discipline to be an effective politician: 'He remains incredibly funny, but he's not interested in detail. Unless you like lots of mind-numbing work, getting on top of budgets, crafting government policy and drafting strategies, you're not doing it.'[89] Livingstone's views are clearly coloured by his electoral defeat by Johnson, especially by the knowledge that his rival will probably get to open the Olympic Games that Livingstone fought so hard to bring to London. However, I was struck by the similarities between this description of Boris's approach and that of another high-profile political figure, who we wrote about in *Crowd Surfing*. Arnold Schwarzenegger, the former bodybuilder, actor and surprisingly successful governor of California, lives what he likes to call an 'improvisational lifestyle'. His style is described as 'relaxed and authentic', which are words you could easily apply to Johnson. Both have been able to appeal to supporters beyond traditional party lines. Their minds may not be tidy, but they seem to thrive amidst the chaos.

---

[88] Tom Peters, *Re-imagine: Business excellence in a disruptive age*, Dorling Kindersley, 2003.
[89] Interview in *Shortlist* magazine, 1 July 2010.

2.2 HARNESSING THE COLLECTIVE IMPULSE

'We're seeing people able to mobilize forms of knowledge and take action, finding other people without needing high-cost professional networks.'

Charles Leadbetter, technology writer and social entrepreneur[90]

In the streets of a small town in Wiltshire, a poignant ritual is being performed by thousands of people with depressing regularity. Wootton Bassett has inadvertently become the focus of the nation's mourning for soldiers killed in the war in Afghanistan. It started out with just a few people standing in silence as the hearses, taking the bodies of soldiers killed in the war from nearby RAF Lyneham to the John Radcliffe Hospital in Oxford, passed through the streets. But it quickly began to attract thousands of people who stand in respectful silence, often for hours, motivated simply by the desire to show solidarity with the suffering of others and demonstrate a shared sense of grief. It has become a collective ritual, made all the more compelling by the fact that it is spontaneous. The townspeople have resisted any attempts to formalize the event, leading the *Daily Telegraph* to describe it as 'a very British version of Arlington, the US cemetery where respect is paid to the fallen. No fuss. No flowers or razzmatazz'.[91]

The author and social media theorist Clay Shirky talks about how historically we haven't been able to achieve organization without some form of institutional structure, typically one built around a hierarchy of authority. The double meaning of the

---

[90] Interview in the *Observer*, 8 August 2010.
[91] *Daily Telegraph*, 7 July 2010.

word 'organization' to describe both the means and the outcome – we need an 'organization' to achieve 'organization' – was beyond challenge. This traditional way of thinking has been subverted by the emergence of online networks which, in Shirky's words, are, 'enabling novel forms of collective action, enabling the creation of collaborative groups that are larger and more distributed than at any other time in history. The scope of work that can be done by non-institutional groups is a profound challenge to the status quo.'[92] Shirky expands on this idea in his latest book, *Cognitive Surplus*,[93] which takes the optimistic view that the aggregation of collective spare time (which is what he means by a cognitive surplus) has the potential to solve many of the world's problems, from highlighting human rights abuses in Kenya to collecting rubbish on the streets in Pakistan. His views echo those of Charles Leadbeater, whose book *We-think: The Power of Mass Creativity*,[94] did much to popularize the idea that amateur creativity, powered by new technology, could solve fundamental social problems, especially in developing countries. It is interesting to debate whether, as Shirky and Leadbeater suggest, new technology has unlocked a latent collective urge – we just needed the arrival of social media to encourage us to work together – or whether it has coincided with a deeper socio-cultural trend.

During the summer of 2009, the British public abandoned any sense of self-restraint and participated in arguably the artistic event of the decade. Artist Antony Gormley invited

---

[92] Clay Shirky, *Here Comes Everybody: The power of organizing without organizations*, Allen Lane, 2008.
[93] Clay Shirky, *Cognitive Surplus: Creativity and generosity in a connected age*, Penguin, 2010.
[94] Charles Leadbeater, *We-think: The power of mass creativity*, Profile Books, 2008.

people to participate in a living artwork in London's Trafalgar Square, which he labelled One & Other. Over a period of 100 days, 2,400 people (one per hour) – selected at random from nearly 35,000 applicants – sat, performed, protested and fed the pigeons on the vacant Fourth Plinth surrounding Nelson's Column. Gormley's project aimed to dramatize the way that authority has been transferred from the ruling elite – the aristocrats and generals who have traditionally occupied the plinths in major public spaces – to the masses. This is a theme that he has explored with his other artworks – the celebration of the anonymous individual. *The Times* described his idea as 'bringing the techniques of reality TV to the world of fine art'. Others described it as 'art for the Facebook generation'. Gormley, despite the fact that he ironically failed to win a place in the ballot for the opportunity to perform on the plinth, was in no doubt about the significance of his artwork: 'Who can be represented in art? How can we make it? How can we experience it? These are questions that have exercised me for years. Whether you see the plinth as a protest or pole-dance platform; studio or stocks; playpen or pulpit; as a frame for interrogation or for meditation, it has provided an open space of possibility for many to test their sense of self and how they might communicate this to a wider world.'[95]

A few of the Fourth Plinth performers decided to take their clothes off, possibly auditioning for another artist, Spencer Tunick, who specializes in mass outbreaks of collective nudity in the name of art. I find it fascinating that thousands of people are willing to take part in Tunick's installations all over the world, from Sydney to Salford. Is it down to exhibitionism, a spirit of collective action or simply the desire to participate in

---

[95] Quoted on the One & Other website, October 2009.

something that you can tell your friends about for years to come? Another artist, Shelley Jackson, in the United States, has demanded an even greater level of collective commitment. In her project 'Skin: a mortal work of art', Jackson has been able to persuade 2,095 complete strangers to agree to have one word of a story tattooed on their bodies. These people will never meet, so their individual sacrifices will never truly make sense. To most people, the participants will simply be displaying a tattoo featuring a random word. One participant described what motivated her to become a living part of the artwork: 'There are only 2,095 of us in the world and as the words die, the story changes. That's the beauty of it. The story itself is a mortal, living, breathing thing.'[96]

Jackson, Gormley and Tunick use the internet to recruit potential collaborators and the Fourth Plinth activities were broadcast via a live webcam, but none of these examples of collective self-expression are dependent on new technology. The social media evangelists like to depict this type of collective behaviour as a by-product of new media technologies, but I would argue that we are dealing with something far more profound and deep-rooted than the emergence of Facebook or Twitter. For a start, it isn't simply confined to the internet. It is all too easy to think of consumer empowerment as simply a web-based phenomenon, but something interesting is also happening beyond the world of social media: public meetings are suddenly all the rage. Not content with simply meeting in a virtual capacity, people increasingly see value in coming together as a physical community – from single-issue protest groups to neighbourhood action groups and residents' associations. The trend was spotted by *The Times Magazine*, with Alan

---

[96] *TrendHunter* magazine, 24 February 2010.

Franks commenting that, 'Just when you thought everything had gone virtual and we'd lost our ability to communicate except by Facebook, back comes the public meeting. Suddenly we're talking again. There are more open gatherings now than 30 years ago, convened for reasons as diverse as the philosophy of Heidegger and the flowering cherry on the corner of Park Crescent that sadly has to go.'[97]

This is potentially even more interesting than the rise of social media. Contributing to an online community is relatively easy – you don't have to move from the computer or mobile keyboard. But getting off your backside and attending a public meeting requires a genuine commitment. The people prepared to do this are likely to be the real change agents within society. In the final months of the Labour administration, Hazel Blears – in a thinly disguised attack on Gordon Brown's clumsy appearance on YouTube – described how using social media was no substitute for real, grassroots political campaigning, such as knocking on doors, setting up a stall in a town centre or debating issues at public meetings. Her comments were seized on by some commentators as an example of political Ludditism, yet Blears wasn't really attacking the party's use of social media, but making the point that political arguments cannot simply be expressed through digital or virtual channels; sometimes, even the most wired, digitally savvy politicians have to go face-to-face with the electorate. This is something that Barack Obama most definitely understands. He may have become the poster child for the use of social media as a campaigning tool, but when he wants to win a political argument – such as over healthcare provision in the US – his instinctive reaction is to start talking face-to-face with the public, at what

[97] *The Times Magazine*, 27 June 2009.

they describe in the US as 'town hall meetings'. The Tea Party movement, which has risen in opposition to many of Obama's policies, is also largely based on a grassroots network of meetings in community halls across the heartland of America.

HARNESSING THE COLLECTIVE SPIRIT

An illustration of the power of informal networks occurred during the winter of 2009. DARPA (the US Defense Advanced Research Projects Agency, which is the research and development arm of the US Department of Defense) conducted an experiment to test the power of social media and specifically its likely utility in the event of a national emergency. It was also designed to celebrate the 40th anniversary of ARPANet, the precursor to the internet. The agency tethered 10 red weather balloons to the ground in different parts of the US and offered a reward of $40,000 to the first team to find all of the locations. It allowed up to nine days for the teams to crack this challenge, but it took a smart group of students at the Massachusetts Institute of Technology's Media Lab – which included experts in computational social science, behavioural economics, social epidemiology, mathematics and computer science – fewer than nine hours to find the locations of all of the balloons, which had been distributed across ten states. They used a classic pyramid scheme, recruiting people across the US to join their search team via a dedicated website, which was launched a few weeks prior to the launch of the DARPA Challenge. Everyone who contributed to finding one of the balloons shared in the prize, so anyone who found one of the 10 balloons received $2,000 (with the same amount going to charity), with the person who invited the individuals who found the balloons receiving $1,000 and the person who invited them receiving $500, and so on.

By the time that the DARPA Challenge was launched, the MIT Media Lab team had assembled a search party of almost 5,000 people. One of the team leaders, Toshiba Professor Alex (Sandy) Pentland said: 'What was most rewarding about this was how we demonstrated the enormous potential of human networking . . . this exercise showed how building the proper incentives into a viral collaboration can quickly harness a large population to work together to address broad societal needs. It has helped us better understand how information spreads and why people cooperate.' Another team member, postdoctorate fellow Riley Crane, revealed how the team was motivated by the desire, 'to understand how to mobilize the vast resources of the human network to face challenges and explore the opportunities that come with living in such a connected world. We believe we have developed a set of tools that can find the proverbial needle in a haystack.'[98]

The challenge of finding 10 large balloons in a country the size of the United States, even if it felt like finding a needle in a haystack, was relatively insignificant compared with the enormous logistical challenge that faced the media in the wake of the MPs' expenses scandal that dominated the British political scene during 2009. When Parliament reluctantly bowed to freedom of information campaigners and allowed details of MPs' expenses to be published, the media was faced with a major problem. How could journalists wade through the mountain of documentation detailing the minutiae of MPs' lives, including claims for light bulbs and moat cleaning, before the story lost momentum? The solution devised by the

---

[98] MIT press release, 10 December 2009.

Guardian newspaper was to call upon the collective time and effort of its readers. As a result, 26,000 amateur investigative reporters went through 22,000 documents in a matter of days. The *Guardian*'s editor, Alan Rusbridger, described this process as 'mutualization', which the paper's social media expert, Meg Pickard, defines as 'getting readers to care about, inform and enhance our coverage'.[99]

The mutualization model is also being used by wildlife and conservation experts. If they want to track the migratory patterns of sharks, establish the relative health of the garden bird population or try to establish whether our bees are dying out, they can call on an army of enthusiastic, amateur volunteers. This type of collective behaviour confounds the economists, who cannot understand how people can be motivated to operate in this way without tangible incentives. Their simplistic view of man as a rational, economic animal doesn't appear to fit the mood of the times, but in the words of David Boyle, the author of *The Public Domain*, 'A surprising amount of useful, creative or expressive activity is generated without any financial incentive at all.'[100] People's motivations are varied, ranging from the desire to demonstrate their expertise to pure altruism.

A similar spirit of altruism brought together a group of transvestites, alpaca farmers and hairdressers – it isn't often you get to include all of them in a sentence – to try to protect the US Gulf Coast during the recent BP oil disaster. In a brilliant example of a loose collaboration – co-ordinated by the Matter of Trust charity – human hair was collected from hair salons in France, Spain, Brazil, Australia, Canada and the US,

---

[99] Quoted in interview with *Brand Republic*, 25 March 2010.
[100] James Boyle, *The Public Domain: Enclosing the commons of the mind*, Yale University Press, 2009.

combined with animal fur from sheep and alpaca farmers and then stuffed into used nylon tights, some of which (naturally the larger ones) were supplied by transvestite group, the Sisters of Perpetual Indulgence. The resulting 'hairy sausages', for that is what they looked like, were then used as booms to help soak up oil leaking from the burst BP well in the Gulf of Mexico.

There are signs that this looser model, built around short-term coalitions of people with shared interests, is beginning to replace traditional institutional charities as the preferred model for grassroots activism. Evidence from the US suggests that single-issue websites are gaining more followers than traditional charity sites. We shouldn't be surprised by this trend. It has never been easier for passionate and creative individuals, with a good idea or a popular cause, and a modicum of technical know-how, to start grassroots campaigns, focused on single issues, that are capable of securing mass support, generating donations and forcing corporations and governments to respond. And the immediacy and novelty of the campaigns developed by these groups makes them feel far more exciting and relevant than many of the ongoing fundraising initiatives implemented by traditional charities. We are now in the era of the 'pop-up cause' in which the dominance of the institutional charities is challenged by short-term, highly focused campaigning groups, that recruit followers to their cause through social media, grab the headlines and then disappear, to be replaced by other groups, with equally short-term goals.

One of my favourite examples of a loose activist model is the Carrotmob. This informal movement, which started in California, uses the power of collective purchasing to persuade businesses to behave in a more socially responsible way. It is people power in its purest form – the corporation agrees to operate more responsibly than its competitors and, in return, the 'mob' agrees to support it with its money. The first Carrot-mob initiative was to reward the off-licence in San Francisco that agreed to spend the highest percentage of its profits on energy efficiency measures. The organizers described this as the opposite of a boycott, arguing that 'there are enough sticks out there. We need a juicy big carrot'[101] – hence the name. This is actually one of the oldest forms of community behaviour – the co-operative or mutual movement – updated for the internet age. And it is yet another example of how the activist community has been quick to spot the opportunities presented by consumer empowerment to form short-term, loose coalitions of diverse groups of people with shared interests. Not surpri-singly, the movement has started to spread around the globe and a number of groups have begun to form in UK cities.

The Carrotmob is driven by a shared belief in the importance of combating behaviour or circumstances that threaten our collective security, such as global warming. Adam Morgan, the author of *Eating the Big Fish*,[102] sees parallels between this type of collective action and the way that traditional folk myths often feature stories of communities rallying together to con-front external monsters. He suggests that institutions should use a figurative monster to rally their supporters: 'a monster is a threat to the larger community. This is what brings the community together: however disparate, divided or simply indolent the community had been up to that point, the presence of a monster brings them together in unity against it. And in fighting the monster, the hero is thus fighting not just

[101] Quoted in the *New York Times*, 19 May 2009.
[102] Adam Morgan, *Eating the Big Fish: How challenger brands can compete against brand leaders*, (Second edition), John Wiley & Sons, 2009.

for themselves, but as the champion of the community as a whole.'[103] Monster creators identified by Morgan include Unilever's Dove brand, with its attack on the damages caused by the global beauty industry to women's sense of self-esteem, and inevitably Virgin: 'Richard Branson's brilliance has been to convince us that his personal business enemies such as BA are in fact monsters, working against the interests of us all.'[104]

In addition to these well-thumbed case studies, Morgan also praises Method – the environmentally friendly cleaning products company. The San Francisco-based firm – with its simple slogan of 'people against dirty' – has built a $200 million business, in a decidedly mundane product category, by dramatizing the 'monster' of toxic chemicals in the home. This has included staging publicity stunts in which Method employees arrive at people's houses to remove toxic cleaning materials, clad in the type of all-encompassing overalls used on toxic-waste sites. This powerful dramatization of the limitations of traditional cleaning products, plus a commitment to innovative and attractive packaging, has helped Method appeal beyond the relatively narrow market for 'green' products and instead reach a broader audience, 'Whether they want to fight the grime on the kitchen floor, take out the toxins in the shower or pummel the bad stuff floating in the world.'[105] The company's co-founder, Adam Lowry, describes the company's proposition as 'green clean for the mainstream'.[106]

---

[103] Talk to the Marketing Society, December 2008.

[104] Adam Morgan, *Eating the Big Fish: How challenger brands can compete against brand leaders*, (Second edition), John Wiley & Sons, 2009.

[105] www.methodproducts.com

[106] 'Environment, health & sustainable business enter the mainstream', Professor Andrea Larson and students from the University of Virginia Darden Graduate School of Business, co-sponsored by IEHN (April 2007).

The technique Morgan describes has been used by political leaders over the centuries to win and safeguard power: identify an external or internal threat – 'Reds under the bed', EU expansion, Weapons of Mass Destruction – to create a shared sense of danger and mobilize community action. The danger comes when these monsters have no basis in reality and are merely phantoms, dreamed up by people who are either pandering to popular prejudice and xenophobia or simply using scare tactics.

MEETING THE CHALLENGE OF COLLECTIVE SELF-EXPRESSION

While some institutions are able to follow Morgan's advice and encourage collective behaviour, others are having to learn to deal with some of the more challenging consequences of what I would characterize as a spirit of collective self-expression. In September 2009 the Great Western Hospital in Swindon, Wiltshire, made the headlines when it found itself at the mercy of a popular craze known as The Lying Down Game. The phenomenon, described by its devotees as 'Parkour . . . for those who can't be arsed', involved people photographing themselves and friends or colleagues lying face down in unusual locations and then posting the results online. The official website features photos of people lying down on escalators, the luggage racks of trains, on the bonnet of police cars, on roofs and fences and even inside a jet engine (which fortunately wasn't in use at the time). The *Daily Mail* described the craze as 'pointless', but that is exactly why it appeals to so many people. It perfectly captures the mildly subversive mood of the times. Seven bored staff working the nightshift at the hospital in Swindon decided to join in the fun, taking photographs of themselves lying down on resuscitation trolleys, ward floors and a heli-pad. No patients were involved in the stunt – they would in any case have already been lying down, so it wouldn't have been particularly unusual – but the staff were subsequently suspended by the hospital authorities, who were simply unsure how else to respond.

Global spirits company Diageo has also found itself the unwitting victim of this spirit of collective self-expression. It discovered that its Smirnoff Ice product was being featured in a new drinking ritual known as 'icing'. As rituals go it was pretty simple – the receiver of a bottle of Smirnoff Ice was expected to down the contents in a single gulp, while being on one knee. It quickly became an internet phenomenon, with videos of 'icings' being posted on the 'bros icing bros' website. The online hype was given extra fuel when a story leaked out about how Facebook founder Mark Zuckerberg had apparently 'iced' a colleague by hiding a bottle in a birthday cake. Diageo, mindful of the need to be seen to be promoting a responsible drinking message, did all it could to discourage the trend, but despite shutting down the website, it was ultimately powerless to prevent it from taking hold.

THE RISE OF CROWDSOURCING

Diageo had to go out of its way to discourage one form of collective creativity, but other institutions are less constrained and are able to harness it to develop new products, services or marketing campaigns. Crowdsourcing – a word coined by *Wired* magazine's Jeff Howe – has become the most commonly used term for this type of activity, which has ranged from dreaming up new flavours of crisp to directing government policy. Credit should also be given to Alvin Toffler, whose book *The Third Wave*, written in 1980, was already anticipating the emergence of 'prosumers', who would eventually become co-creators, involved in both product design and production. Crowdsourcing has started to mature as an organizational or marketing technique, adding tangible value to new product development and the handling of customer enquiries. Many institutions have discovered the benefits of harnessing group wisdom and collective effort. Research by McKinsey has indicated that 70 per cent of executives claim that their companies regularly create value through the use of web-based communities.[107] The management consultancy has estimated that using existing customer communities to help other customers solve problems – an approach increasingly taken by many consumer technology businesses – costs around 10 per cent of the cost of using a traditional call centre to handle customer enquiries. It has also analysed the effectiveness of one of the highest profile brand communities, P&G's Vocalpoint panel, a global network of influential mothers, set up to provide the company with feedback on new products and services. McKinsey estimated that product revenues in countries in which Vocalpoint members are active, were twice the level of those without an active community.[108]

Crowdsourcing may sound like a completely loose way of sourcing new suggestions and ideas, but it only works well when given some structure, plus the right technology platforms

---

[107] 'How companies are benefiting from Web 2.0: McKinsey Global Survey Results', *McKinsey Quarterly*, August 2009.

[108] Both estimates taken from 'Clouds, big data & smart assets: Ten tech-enabled business trends to watch', *McKinsey Quarterly*, August 2010.

and most importantly an understanding of how to build and nurture a collaborative culture. McKinsey has highlighted how: 'Some companies neglect the up-front research needed to identify potential participants who have the right skill sets and will be motivated to participate over the longer term' and argued that 'Since co-creation is a two-way process, companies must also provide feedback to stimulate continuing participation and commitment.'[109] Co-creation or crowdsourcing initiatives also require some form of management. Few institutions can spare the time to wade through a mountain of inappropriate or irrelevant suggestions, in the hope of finding one creative nugget, which is why running a crowdsourced project takes as much effort, if not more, than a conventional one. You also have to allow for the subversive streak that characterizes much of our online culture. Given the opportunity, the public will invariably try to undermine or game the system, so when the Canadian teenage pop star Justin Bieber asked his fans to suggest the country he should visit on his next tour, the online community took great pleasure in putting North Korea at the top of the list. Chevrolet experienced a similar problem when an attempt to crowdsource ideas for an ad for its Tahoe SUV became a platform for different activist groups to attack the company's record on climate change and to express anti-American sentiments.

As well as providing a clear brief, that defines clear parameters for what is required, the best crowdsourcing initiatives provide a facility for those involved to comment on and rate other people's suggestions as well as submit their own. In this way the wider community is involved in both the creation and

---

[109] 'Clouds, big data & smart assets: Ten tech-enabled business trends to watch', *McKinsey Quarterly*, August 2010.

the selection of ideas. Intellectual property issues also need to be addressed. Who receives royalties for the chosen idea – the originator or the institution managing the initiative? Phil Knight may have famously paid Carolyn Davidson only $35 to design the original Nike Swoosh in the early 70s,[110] but these days even amateur creatives are pretty sophisticated when it comes to generating revenue from their ideas. There are a variety of models that can be adopted, ranging from forcing people to waive all of their rights, to the sharing of revenue, but the critical point is that the rules need to be specified and agreed in advance.

Mutualization and crowdsourcing represent loose thinking in action and a demonstration of how formal, tight institutional structures are no longer the only means of achieving commercial success or social progress. The future appears to lie with informal coalitions of people or groups, built around a shared and often temporary interest in flexible organizational models able to leverage what appears to be a latent desire to create, contribute and collaborate. It is 15 years since Robert Putnam wrote the highly influential book, *Bowling Alone*,[111] highlighting how we were becoming increasingly disconnected from family, friends and neighbours and disengaged from the political process. He described how the lack of what he termed 'social capital' was undermining our relationships and communities and pointed to a decline in formal religious observance, community volunteering and membership of trade unions and PTAs as evidence of a lack of civic engagement. It may be that we have finally rediscovered the urge to reconnect,

---

[110] He subsequently gave her a diamond Swoosh ring and some Nike stock.
[111] Robert Putnam, *Bowling Alone: The collapse and revival of American community*, Simon & Schuster, 2001.

partly virtually – through the power of social media – but also through an interest in communal activities. All over the world, the number of people attending sports and music events, taking part in mass participation runs and attending public meetings is on the increase. Social media likes to take the credit, but it is the desire for shared communal experiences that is at its heart.

The power of loose, informal networks – such as MIT's DARPA Challenge team or the Carrotmob – would appear to be almost without limit: they can solve some of society's most difficult social problems, reinvigorate the democratic process or devise break-through creative ideas. They can do all of this, and more, by tapping into people's innate desire to become part of a larger, collective endeavour. But more importantly, the speed at which they can emerge and the often unpredictable agenda that they follow, all too often dramatizes the deficiencies of the tight, bureaucratic structures that have to deal with them. In the words of marketing writer, Mark Earls: 'For those of us who like clear lines, and black and whites, collaboration presents all kinds of blurry emotional and practical difficulties. Collaboration is messy, often unpredictable and, with the exception of those who insist on retaining control, more fun than the old world. But to be honest, I'm not sure we have a choice.'[112]

---

[112] *AdMap* magazine, May 2010.

2.3 X+Y = A PERFECT GENERATIONAL STORM

'We've done this before: Each and every time, a new generation has risen up and done what's needed to be done. Today we are called once more, and it is time for our generation to answer that call.'

Barack Obama's Presidential Candidacy
Announcement, 10 February 2007[113]

In July 2007 the Mayor of Paris, Bertrand Delanoë, launched the *vélo libre* or velib bicycle rental programme. Building on the success of similar schemes in Lyon and La Rochelle, the scheme is now the largest in the world, providing 20,000 bicycles and over 1,600 rental stations throughout central Paris. While commuters enjoy the convenience of a pleasant cycle ride through the streets of Paris or the terrifying experience of trying to navigate the roads surrounding l'Arc de Triomphe, younger Parisians have chosen to put the bicycles to an alternative use. They are performing stunts – on what were originally described (somewhat naively) as 'damage-resistant' bicycles – filming their best moves and posting them on YouTube. The craze, which has become known as Velib Extreme, has generated numerous online videos, including footage of riders taking the bikes down the steps in Montmartre and into Métro stations. The recent introduction of a similar scheme in London will almost certainly be greeted with the same creative response from the city's youth.

A similarly subversive streak, albeit less dangerous, has encouraged a group of enterprising economics students at

---

[113] Barack Obama's Candidacy Announcement: Springfield, Illinois, 10 February 2007.

Bristol University to work together to change the balance of power in the job recruitment market. They had observed how interviewers from the major companies involved in the annual recruitment 'milk round' and universities looking to select postgraduates, tended to ask the same questions of potential candidates. They responded by creating a website, www. whatwilltheyask.co.uk, giving potential recruits the inside track on the recruitment strategies used by different companies and the types of question they would be asked.

This is the new generation that is shaping our popular culture and entering the workplace. Peter Gilroy, CEO of Kent County Council, has described how, 'The next genera-tion, as natives of the digital world, will have revolutionary implications for politics, the public sector and the way we do business. The citizen will drive change and bring social revolution, not evolution'.[114] His view of this new generation's political inclinations is open to debate. Evgeny Morozov, Yahoo fellow at Georgetown University, cautions against the assumption that a new generation of 'digital natives' – the teenagers and twenty-somethings brought up in a digital world – are more likely to become political activists. He argues that younger web users are more interested in cyber hedonism than cyber activism.[115] They are invariably too busy having fun to worry about the need for social change.

Every generation has its label. This one has been christened Generation Y, for no better reason than they followed Genera-tion X, which was the commonly used label to describe the group of people born in the 1960s and 70s. MTV has come up

---

[114] 'Capitalising on Complexity, Insights from the Global Chief Executive Officer Study', IBM, 2009.
[115] Speech to the RSA, 22 September 2009.

with an alternative moniker: the Cyborg Generation, or Cyber-Gens for short. Described by *Marketing* magazine as 'the generation of tweeting, texting, social networking-obsessed youth',[116] this latest incarnation of the 16–25-year-old demographic is driven by a potent mix of self-expression and collective action, combined with the mildly subversive streak that helped put Rage Against the Machine at the top of the Christmas pop charts in the UK. It refuses to respect or defer to traditional figures of authority and expertise, whether they are major business recruiters or the public transport operators of Paris. Opinions are there to be challenged and as far as they are concerned, their viewpoint always merits attention. A few minutes spent reading the often anonymous comments accompanying most of the material on YouTube demonstrate how this group is certainly not afraid to voice an opinion.

The technological revolution has also created a culture of narcissism among this generation, characterized, like all narcissistic traits, by a high level of self-importance, a sense of entitlement and a confidence in its unique abilities. Tim Adams, writing in the *Observer*, came up with a simple explanation for this phenomenon: 'A world that constantly reflects back to you your own wishes, through a computer that seems to be your friend, will inevitably enhance your sense of self and the unwarranted belief that your views have weight and authority.'[117] This trait was explored in detail by Jean Twenge in her book *Generation Me*,[118] in which she described America's youth as 'more confident, assertive, entitled – and

---

[116] *Marketing Week*, 22 September 2009.
[117] *Observer*, 6 December 2009.
[118] Jean Twenge, *Generation Me: Why today's young Americans are more confident, assertive, entitled – and more miserable than ever before*, Free Press, 2007.

more miserable than ever before'. Twenge, who is a psychology professor at San Diego State University, has also been involved in a research study which revealed that 57 per cent of young people in the US agreed with the statement that, 'People in my generation use social networking sites for self-promotion, narcissism and attention seeking' and almost 40 per cent agreed that 'being self-promoting, narcissistic, overconfident, and attention-seeking is helpful for succeeding in a competitive world.'[119]

This narcissism, when combined with the strange sense of confusion between the private and public space that defines this generation's use of social media, can lead to problems. Azeem Rafiq used to be the captain of the England Under-19 cricket team, until he decided to express his frustrations with his coach, John Abrahams, through the public forum that is Twitter. Whether the result of ignorance or stupidity, his use of highly offensive language in a series of tweets, to complain about being dropped and disciplined for what the ECB described as 'inappropriate conduct', had predictable consequences. He was suspended from all forms of the game during the summer of 2010, the number of people following him on Twitter increased by 800 per cent – and hopefully he learnt that you shouldn't say anything about people in social media that you wouldn't say directly to their faces. Just to prove that social media naivety isn't restricted to the younger generation, England's struggling star batsman, Kevin Pietersen, was censured and fined for issuing a similarly profanity-laden tweet when he learnt that he was to be dropped from the England One Day team in the series against Pakistan.

Rafiq's Twitter-based criticisms were a direct challenge to

---

[119] Youth Pulse research, commissioned by SDSU (August 2009).

the authority of his coach. For this generation, authority has been dispersed: it doesn't come automatically with seniority or experience, but has to be earned. They will also take great pleasure in subverting any attempts by authority figures to silence them. One of my recent stories involved Lebron James, a Nike-sponsored basketball star, being out-witted by a college student called Jordan Crawford during a university skills academy. In a one-on-one challenge, Crawford outmanoeuvred James and celebrated by scoring a slam-dunk. Amateur footage, recorded by spectators on their camera phones, began to circulate online within hours, alongside claims that Nike was trying to confiscate official film of the event. Over a million YouTube views later, Nike found itself facing a rare PR crisis that didn't reflect well on the company or its star player.

Cynicism may be their default setting, but unlike previous youth generations, this doesn't necessarily make them antagonistic towards big brands. Not for them the No Logo[120] mantra, taken up by Generation X, that defined all major brands as innately exploitative and evil and legitimized the ritual trashing of Starbucks or McDonald's shopfronts during any urban protests. Having grown up during one of the longest periods of sustained economic growth and been exposed to an explosion of product innovation, especially in the technology sector, they have a strong materialistic streak. Brands such as Apple, *X Factor* and Abercrombie & Fitch play a key role in their lives. They give them a sense of identity and belonging, within a ready-made community of like-minded individuals. This is the reason why Coca-Cola's Facebook page – created

---

[120] After Naomi Klein's book *No Logo: Solutions for a sold planet*, Flamingo, 2000.

by two Coca-Cola fans and operated largely autonomously – is now the second most popular site on Facebook. But it doesn't make them an easy or passive target – their 'bullshit detector' is set to max and they are quick to criticize any brand behaviour that they consider patronizing or just plain boring. Get it right – like the people who dreamt up the Rage Against the Machine Christmas number one campaign and Barack Obama's campaign team – and they will reward you with their loyalty and money, just so long as you don't take them for granted. In the words of Rage Against the Machine's 'Killing in the Name', 'F*** You. I won't do what you tell me.'

A booming economy has also given them high expectations of levels of service and convenience. For a generation that has grown up with the instantaneous answers provided by Google and Wikipedia, waiting for anything seems unacceptable. Rory Sutherland, an experienced creative director and president of the UK's Institute of Professionals in Advertising, admits to being bewildered by what he describes as 'the insane new expectation of speed' among younger consumers who have grown up in the instant-click world of the internet: 'When they send an email, for instance, or text a client, they are reduced to complete befuddlement if they do not get an answer within twenty minutes – or at most an hour. They start emailing and texting incessantly. To older clients, this is unbelievably annoying. To the young, this is normal behaviour.' Sutherland also quotes a 21-year-old as saying that, 'The trouble with McDonald's is it's too bloody slow.' This often irrational need for speed – is young people's time that valuable? – has become one of the defining characteristics of modern society and has also left most institutions in the slow lane. This is the first generation to truly operate in real time, in the sense that they demand and expect instant access, instant responses and instant gratification. MTV described it as 'living life through shortcuts'.[121] It is an attitude that appears to be becoming contagious, with the public as a whole now demanding that all institutions respond almost instantaneously to their demands. This is a frightening thought given the glacial pace at which most organizations make decisions.

We are also dealing with a generation brought up in a culture of ripping, sharing and remixing and comfortable with the rough-and-ready look of most of the consumer-generated content they see on YouTube. High production values are no longer seen as a signifier of high quality. This reduces the competitive advantages typically enjoyed by large companies or brands with access to high production budgets and means that many of the most viewed pieces of content on the internet are produced by amateurs, rather than professional creative teams. Commercial organizations are being forced to rethink the way that they present themselves. Generation Y don't want and certainly don't trust the glossy, crafted image of the company that appears in the brochure, preferring to deal with something a bit ragged around the edges that they can adapt themselves and then, if the content is good enough, pass it on to someone else. As a recent focus group attendee told me, 'If it isn't worth sharing, it isn't any good.' This has become the new test for any creative idea – is it good enough to share?

The generation that preceded the current under-25 demographic, Generation X, was often derided as the arch slackers. They were memorably depicted by Douglas Coupland, in his book *Generation X*,[122] as doing 'pointless jobs done grudgingly

---

[121] MTV Generation v.2 report, September 2009.
[122] Douglas Coupland, *Generation X: Tales for an accelerated culture*, Abacus, 1996.

to little applause'. Generation Y may be more commercially oriented, especially when it comes to their consumption of brands, but they appear no more enamoured with the prospect of work. A survey by organizational change experts, TalentSmoothie, among people born after 1980 underlined this point.[123] It highlighted how this generation reject their parents' work-dominated lives and are quite happy to walk away from any role that doesn't match their aspirations. The current economic recession and shrinking job market are likely to shatter their confidence in their ability to always find alternative means of employment, but a generation that has become accustomed to its gap years and flexible working will find it difficult to adjust. A YouGov poll for the Conservative Centre for Policy Studies[124] showed that 31 per cent of what they described as 'Generation Y mothers' did not want to work at all, finding more satisfaction in their roles as carers, partners, community members and above all mothers, rather than fighting their way up the corporate ladder.

Those willing to embrace the world of work have a heightened expectation of how they should be treated. Flexible working times and locations are particularly important, as is the provision of constant and immediate feedback. The TalentSmoothie survey revealed that 85 per cent of Gen Y want to spend 30–70 per cent of their time working from home, which might help to reduce congestion during the rush hour, but will pose a challenge for most managers. The survey also listed the criteria essential to Gen Y as a good work/life balance, personal development, an exciting job and motivational

---

[123] http://www.talentsmoothie.com/articles/2008/10/generation-y-what-they-want-from-work
[124] Published in October 2009.

management. The report's authors rightly pointed out that these priorities are actually shared by most demographic groups. The difference is that this generation, driven by a sense of entitlement, is not afraid to ask for them.

Many of these new entrants to the workforce believe, with some justification, that they have a better understanding of the new social technologies than their so-called bosses. In his book *Grown-Up Digital*, which is a celebration of the technological skills of a group he christened 'the net generation', Don Tapscott described how, 'Young people have a natural affinity for technology that seems uncanny. They instinctively turn first to the net to communicate, understand, learn, find and do many things.'[125] And if they can't immediately find what they want on the net, in the spirit of *Who Wants to be a Millionaire?*, they will simply phone (text, email or tweet) a friend. They regard knowledge as something to be shared among their peers, rather than kept to oneself, and see collaboration as a natural state of affairs, whether solving problems, fine-tuning ideas or creating richer experiences.

Accommodating the interests and aspirations of the technologically savvy Gen Y is a particular challenge within the IT industry. Writing in *Business Strategy Review* about Microsoft's strategy for accommodating Gen Y, Julian Birkinshaw and Stuart Crainer described this task as 'a challenge to conventional management'.[126] They summarized Microsoft's solution as applying 'Theory Y to Generation Y', which meant an emphasis on freedom and trust, while individual creativity and responsibility were encouraged. Birkinshaw and Crainer quote one of

---

[125] Don Tapscott, *Grown-Up Digital: How the Net generation is changing your world*, McGraw-Hill Professional, 2008.
[126] *Business Strategy Review*, Winter 2008.

the Microsoft senior managers: 'We're giving people the latitude to go off and do their own thing. We trust them to do their regular jobs and to experiment, innovate and have fun. We're developing a level of trust where there's no required accountability that you need to log your time or provide an example of what you did during that day when you work at home.' And all the evidence would suggest that this approach, geared to the Gen Y mindset, is paying dividends within Microsoft, with productivity improving and record levels of employee retention.

In a fascinating article in *BusinessWeek* on the rise of this generation in China, Nandani Lynton and Kirsten Høgh Thøgersen remind us that this is a global phenomenon.[127] The self-confidence of Gen Y in China is exacerbated by the single child policy, which has ensured that all of the parent's attention and money has been lavished upon them. Lynton and Høgh Thøgersen described how their willingness to speak up and assert their opinions presents a major problem for their more typically reticent managers: 'The young want to take the initiative and share ideas but lack experience. Their immediate bosses at the middle level feel squeezed, not respected and unable to deal with their young subordinates.' They provide a really interesting metaphor for the perfect management style to accommodate the needs of Gen Y as 'like a kung-fu master who stays in the background, teaching through small hints' rather than simply issuing instructions.

---

[127] *BusinessWeek*, 16 February 2010.

GENERATION X GROWS UP

Some of my first bosses, when I entered the workplace in the late 1980s, had fought in the Vietnam War. As young men they had taken command of patrol boats and helicopter gunships, which makes modern gap years look pretty pathetic. It is hardly surprising that this experience shaped their view of how to organize people and get things done. It would be an exaggeration to suggest that they were all devotees of a command and control mindset. They included many different personality types. One of the senior managers who had spent his early twenties commanding a patrol boat up the Mekong Delta was a passionate believer in the importance of a democratic approach to management and emotional intelligence as a leadership trait. But there was a sense that this generation found comfort in hierarchy and structure, or at least were prepared to tolerate it.

It is always dangerous to make too many sweeping generalizations about generations. The baby boomer ethos is as much characterized by the hippie ideals of freedom and equality, as it is by that generation's wartime experiences. Equally, the boomer generation includes mavericks, such as Richard Branson, who espouse a much looser philosophy when it comes to business. Some argue in favour of an intermediate generational definition, separating baby boomers from Generation X. 'Generation Jones' is the label used by social commentator Jonathan Pontell for people born between 1955 and 67, filling the space 'between the original Glastonbury revellers and the Acid House ravers, between Twiggy and Kate Moss, and between *Abbey Road* and *Wonderwall*'.[128] He

---

[128] Quoted in the *Independent*, 3 May 2010.

may have a valid point – there are endless ways in which different demographic groups can be segmented – but it doesn't change the fact that there is an undeniable sense of a post-boomer mindset. When David Cameron described Gordon Brown as 'an analogue politician in a digital age',[129] he wasn't simply criticizing the shortcomings of his opponent, but trying to position himself as an embodiment of the post-boomer, technically savvy leader that Britain needed in the 21st century. Barack Obama did something similar with John McCain in the US presidential campaign, juxtaposing his post-Cold War world viewpoint with that of McCain, the grizzled Vietnam War veteran. In fact, from the very beginning of his career, Obama seemed determined to challenge the thinking and political outlook of the previous generation: 'I decided . . . that in style and attitude I, too, could be a rebel, unconstrained by the received wisdom of the over-thirty crowd.'[130] Sarah Palin has also built much of her grassroots appeal on the basis of her willingness to challenge the boomer hierarchy within Washington.

A generation that holds up Google's Larry Page and Sergey Brin or Zappos' Tony Hsieh as its role models, likes to think of itself as more casual (both in attitude and dress sense), more flexible and, I would argue, looser, than its predecessor heading for a comfortable retirement. It is this self-image that is the most important behavioural driver. Generational descriptions or labels tend to be self-fulfilling, so if you are told you are part of a particular group and given a set of positive adjectives associated with it – 'informal', 'pragmatic', 'creative', etc. –

---

[129] David Cameron's response to Gordon Brown's Budget Statement, 22 March 2006.
[130] Barack Obama, *The Audacity of Hope: Thoughts on reclaiming the American dream*, Canongate Books, 2008.

you are bound to start thinking of yourself in those terms. The post-boomer mantra is adaptability, collaboration, consensus and dialogue, rather than what they like to depict as the boomer's faith in command and control. This generational shift is not lost on William W. George, a professor of management at Harvard Business School and director of both ExxonMobil and Goldman Sachs. In an interview in *Forbes* magazine, he says, 'We are going through a massive generational change in leadership. We baby boomers were raised in an era coming out of two world wars and the Depression that our parents had experienced. We didn't live through that, but our parents' experience was very real to us. From that we developed a command-and-control mentality of how to run an organization. The great corporations of the world in the 1950s and '60s were command-and-control organizations. With this new century, that concept of command and control has totally gone out, because employees today are knowledge workers, they have options, and they don't stay around. Most important, they're looking for meaning, not just money.'[131]

Tamara Erickson, author of *What's Next, Gen X*,[132] believes that the formative experiences of this generation during the 1970s and 80s have given them the skills necessary to thrive in this new world. 'Today's businesses are facing new, unpredictable challenges. What we've thought of as leadership skills – setting direction, having the answers, controlling performance, running a tight ship – are less relevant in an environment of constant change. Increasingly, leadership is about creating a context for innovation and inclusion in the face of ambiguity

---

[131] *Forbes* magazine, 19 July 2010.
[132] Tamara Erickson, *What's Next, Gen X: Keeping up, moving ahead and getting the career you want*, Harvard Business School Press, 2009.

and the unexpected. I believe Generation X is up for that challenge.'[133] They have lived through the economic and social upheaval of the recession in the 1980s, which ended the idea of a job for life. Equally, the civil and sexual rights battles, won during the 1960s, ensure that they are the first truly multicultural generation, with an appreciation of the value of diversity, sexuality, ethnicity and also opinion. The end of the simplicities and certainties of the Cold War, and its replacement by a confused and fragmented political landscape, has given them a much more nuanced and complex understanding of the world around them and a recognition that it is not always easy to differentiate the good guys from the bad. They may not be 'digital natives', but they have had to learn how to adapt to unprecedented advancements in new technology. When I started working in the mid- to late 1980s, the fax machine was considered advanced technology and mobile telephony was something you only saw on *Star Trek*. Within 20 years, mainly through a process of trial and error, my generation has become digitally competent and occasionally confident. Tamara Erickson has also emphasized how having two working parents – our mothers were the first generation to enter the workforce in any meaningful way – has also taught us to be self-reliant.

The annual TED gathering provides a platform for the post-boomer view of the world. In 1984 an eclectic group of experts in technology, entertainment and design (hence the name) gathered together in Monterey, California, to gawp at the latest technology and share ideas. One of the first products they saw during this initial gathering was the original Apple Mackintosh computer. Since that time, TED's scope and appeal has broadened, both geographically – there are now

---

[133] Quoted in *Fast Company* magazine, 6 August 2010.

satellite events in Oxford and Mysore – and also in terms of its audience. It now attracts a diverse group of technologists, writers, artists, behavioural scientists and business leaders, who gather to listen to leading-edge thinkers, review new technologies and debate new ideas. In the words of the *Economist*, 'There are not many conferences at which a talk by Bill Gates on preventing malaria and educating America's disadvantaged school children would be followed by a discourse on how internet pornography is changing relations between the sexes.'[134] The *San Franciso Chronicle* describe how, 'Spending a few days at the TED conference simultaneously taxes the brain and inspires the mind. The world's most pressing problems are on constant display, counterbalanced by mind-boggling innovations. It's a marketplace for ideas. A place where issues are discussed and consensus formed.'[135] It was typical that Al Gore chose the TED conference in 2006 to unveil his film *An Inconvenient Truth*.

Compared to the annual gathering of business and financial elites at the World Economic Forum in Davos, TED is undeniably loose. It champions an eclectic range of topics, is driven by a sense of social mission, refuses to abide by the convention of nominating keynote speakers and doesn't provide a VIP area – so that Hollywood film stars have to rub shoulders with obscure academics. Since 2001, TED has been owned by British publisher and social activist Chris Anderson, who has focused the collective minds of the TED membership on finding solutions to some of the world's most intractable social problems. The organization's philosophy is simple: 'We believe passionately in the power of ideas to change attitudes,

---

[134] *Economist*, 12 February 2009.
[135] *San Francisco Chronicle*, 7 February 2009.

lives and ultimately, the world.'[136] It may be a social enterprise, but Anderson has created a huge money-making machine – the tickets to its four-day conferences cost over £4,000. To qualify for a ticket, you have to answer a series of questions on the registration form to demonstrate that you have something educational or inspirational to contribute.

TED has also created a prize fund for 'an exceptional individual' who receives $100,000 and the opportunity to make 'One Wish to Change the World'. The winner of the 2010 TED prize was Jamie Oliver, to support his campaign against unhealthy diets. Previous winners have included Bono and Bill Clinton. Oliver's wish, which is designed to encourage the TED Fellows to contribute their ideas, time, contacts and money for his campaign, is to 'create a strong, sustainable movement to educate every child about food, inspire families to cook again and empower people everywhere to fight obesity'. He has already shown, with his campaign to improve the health and nutritional quality of school meals in the UK, that his simple message can force governments to change their policies. Backed by the TED network, a passionate and compelling personality, such as Jamie Oliver, has the opportunity to be a far more effective force for social change than the traditional campaigning institutions.

Rather than tightly controlling the TED franchise, Anderson and his colleagues have been driven by a spirit of what they describe as 'radical openness'. Video content from the conferences is given away for free, while community groups, schools and event organizers around the world can be granted a licence to host their own mini-TED conferences – called TEDx – in the spirit of the TED mission of 'ideas worth spreading'. This

---

[136] www.ted.com

doesn't mean that the TED Fellows give up all control of their brand – the licences come with a wide range of conditions, which require event organizers to meet an agreed set of responsibilities, from gaining TED approval for any local sponsorship deals to providing detailed feedback – but it represents a very different business model than that typically adopted by conference and event organizers.

We are witnessing what I would characterize as a perfect generational storm, in which groups at the top and bottom of our major institutions are driving the adoption of loose thinking and looser ways of working. In a sense, it should be a perfect partnership. Both generations share a belief in the importance of collaboration, creativity and flexibility and a rejection of what they would describe as the stereotypical command-and-control mindset. Between them, they have the capability to transform the business and political landscape, embrace new patterns of consumer behaviour and harness the extraordinary power of new technology.

2.4 THE CONNECTED CONSUMER MEETS THE DISCONNECTED CORPORATION

'Digital communications is a destabilizing force in a bureaucratic environment. And I am sitting right in the middle of a bureaucratic environment.'

The response of a senior corporate communications director, quoted in a report by recruitment specialists Watson Helsby[137]

An angry and empowered individual, with access to the internet, now has the ability to force even the most powerful corporations to back down. In one of the most famous examples of recent years, Canadian songwriter Dave Carroll, armed with a catchy protest song and a YouTube video, was able to mount a global publicity attack on United Airlines. Carroll had spent almost a year trying to persuade the airline to compensate him for the damage done by its baggage handlers to one of his prized guitars. While in transit at Chicago's O'Hare airport, Carroll describes how, 'a woman sitting behind me, not aware that we were musicians, cried out: "My God, they're throwing guitars out there."'[138] After trying and failing to get a satisfactory response from the airline through the usual customer service routes, Carroll and his band, Sons of Maxwell, posted a country music-style protest song on YouTube. In his words, 'It occurred to me that I had been fighting a losing battle all this time and that fighting over this at all was a waste of time. The system is designed to frustrate affected customers into giving up their

---

[137] 'Digital Communications and Social Media – the challenges facing the PR industry', Watson Helsby report, 2010.
[138] www.davecarrollmusic.com

claims and United is very good at it but I realized then that as a songwriter and traveling musician I wasn't without options.'[139] Within hours the appropriately titled 'United Breaks Guitars' was viewed by almost six million people all over the world.

The PR people at United responded promptly to Carroll's musical protest. They issued a statement within hours describing the film as a 'unique learning opportunity'. They issued a further statement via Twitter, which read: 'This has struck a chord [with] us [I'm not sure if they meant this as a pun, I suspect not] and we've contacted him directly to make it right.' They also committed to using the film internally 'to promote better customer service' and Carroll was offered compensation. This is textbook crisis management practice – apologize, solve the problem and claim that you will learn from the experience; the media will eventually get bored with the story and you can move on. Unfortunately, United hadn't allowed for the fact that Carroll, hitherto an obscure singer, had now been given a global platform to perform his material. A second video appeared on YouTube and then a third. It is even being marketed as the 'United Breaks Guitars Trilogy' on Carroll's website.

It is a shame that Steven Slater didn't work for United Airlines, as I am sure he would have come up with a suitably dramatic response to Dave Carroll. Slater, an air steward with US airline JetBlue, made the headlines in August 2010 when, after a row with a passenger on arrival at New York's JFK airport, he swore over the intercom, grabbed a couple of beers and exited using the plane's emergency slide. He was arrested and charged with criminal mischief, reckless endangerment and trespassing, but his actions turned him into

[139] www.davecarrollmusic.com

something of a folk hero. Facebook groups were formed in his honour, fellow flight stewards started raising money to pay for his legal fees and there is already talk of him joining the chat-show circuit. Unfortunately, without Slater's sense of drama, the people at United didn't know what to do. They hadn't been able to move on. And Carroll's very public protest even appeared to be undermining the company's share price, which dropped by around 10 per cent at the height of the media storm that accompanied the first video. Carroll continued to set the agenda and YouTube gave him a platform to reach millions. As well as boosting his performing career, his well-publicized problems with United have given him a second career as a conference speaker on customer service issues, plus an endorsement contract with the manufacturer of sturdy guitar cases. Meanwhile, United's reputation was dragged further into the mire.

I have discussed this case study during numerous workshops and asked people how they would have responded, had they been leading the United Airlines communications effort. Without exception, they will ask, why didn't United make their own video? Why let Carroll get all the attention? Why not get a bunch of United staff together to perform their own apology song? It would demonstrate United's human side; no longer would they be the anonymous, incompetent corporation, but a business made up of real people trying to do the right thing. This was the approach adopted by Asda when they faced their own YouTube-based challenge. A disgruntled former employee created a video which showed him throwing eggs, letting off fire extinguishers and messing around with raw chicken behind the scenes at one of the stores and sent a copy to the local papers. Not surprisingly, the media picked up the story as an example of corporate negligence and poor employee management and it soon began appearing on YouTube. Asda chose to tear up the crisis management rulebook. Instead of issuing a contrite public statement from someone in a suit, the company enlisted workers from the Preston store featured in the original video to make their own film, in which they apologized to customers, expressed their distress at the damage that had been done to their store's reputation and promised that nothing similar would ever be allowed to happen again. This direct appeal to their customers, made via YouTube, was far more compelling and credible than anything that could have come out of the boardroom.

Toyota adopted a similar tactic in the wake of the crisis surrounding its global product recall, although not until after they had been widely criticized for the slowness of their initial response. It issued a series of commercials featuring real employees talking about their commitment to ensuring the high quality of the cars, accompanied by the line 'Your Toyota is My Toyota'. My one criticism would be that the highly polished nature of the commercials made this appeal to customers look far less authentic and credible than the rough, amateurish video put together by the employees at the Asda store in Preston.

Companies have also been blindsided by the way in which social media has empowered their internal critics. The confusion between private and public space which characterizes many people's attitudes towards social media has encouraged a remarkable level of indiscretion among employees, whether it is revealing a less attractive side to their character to a potential employer or, in an increasing number of cases, criticizing the customers who ultimately pay their wages. Tesco employees were discovered on Facebook describing their customers as 'rude, smelly and stupid', while Waitrose employees used words like 'Pikey skanks' to describe some of their less affluent shoppers. Virgin Atlantic fired 13 cabin crew for describing passengers as 'chavs', suggesting the planes were infested with cockroaches and criticizing safety standards.

These are all classic examples of how social media has transformed people's behaviour, expectations and ability to express themselves. People now expect to be able to pose questions, highlight problems, debate issues and share ideas with institutions across multiple communications platforms and in real time, all of which dramatizes the structural, organizational and cultural weaknesses of the organizations that have to deal with them. The emergence of social media has held up a mirror to businesses, political parties and other institutions, and the image it has shown them is not particularly attractive. The connected consumer has come face to face with the disconnected corporation.

Acres of media coverage and hours of conference speeches have been devoted to the power of Facebook or the wonders of Twitter. The growth figures are compelling. Facebook has recently celebrated its 500 millionth user, which means that a staggering 7.4 per cent of the world's population is now connected through a common social media platform. It took five years for Facebook to attract the first 100 million, but only five months to attract the last 100 million, leading the social network's founder Mark Zuckerberg to claim that it is 'almost a guarantee' that it will hit the one billion figure sometime soon.[140] Meanwhile, the Twitter microblogging network is attracting more than 300,000 new users across the world every day.

---

[140] Speech at Cannes Lions International Advertising Festival, 23 June 2010.

This does not mean that the road ahead will be entirely smooth. The technology research specialist Gartner has been using its 'hype cycle' model since 1995, to track the introduction of new technologies. All innovations move through five distinct phases in the Gartner model: an initial 'technology trigger' is followed by 'the peak of inflated expectations', when the enthusiasm and hyperbole is at its most intense. This is followed by the 'trough of disillusionment', when the technology inevitably fails to meet the exaggerated expectations of its launch phase. A gradual recovery, through the 'slope of enlightenment', ultimately leads to a situation in which the technology becomes stable or mature, its benefits become broadly accepted and it is adopted by mainstream consumers: a stage appropriately described by Gartner as a 'plateau of productivity'.

Social media is right at the top of Gartner's 'peak of inflated expectations' – the breathless hyperbole is at its most intense; social media is being presented as the solution for all of society's ills, a means of reinvigorating the democratic process and a panacea for all business problems. In the mainstream business world, confidence is steadily growing in the ability of social media to deliver a broad range of communications objectives, from tracking consumer sentiment about a company or issue and providing advance warning of impending problems, to rallying supporters and facilitating their involvement in product, policy or service developments. It is a state of affairs all too familiar for those of us old enough to remember the first internet boom of the mid- to late 1990s. One of the more insightful commercials of the time was commissioned by IBM. It portrayed a stereotypical group of shirt-sleeved businessmen sitting around a boardroom table, reviewing the latest report from their IT department. One said, 'Our IT guys said we need to be online.' 'Why?' another remarked. 'They didn't say'. This was typical of the mood of the times – just get your business online and don't worry about what you are trying to achieve – but is also all too typical of the herd-like response of many institutions to the emergence of social media. The cry to their communications people is to 'get us on Facebook, write me a blog and start tweeting'. In most cases, they have no clear objectives; it is simply enough to be seen to be embracing this new media platform.

There will inevitably be a crash in the fortunes of social media, as businesses begin to question the value they have derived from their initial investments. We saw this in the aftermath of the first internet boom, when the hundreds of thousands of pounds invested in state-of-the-art websites was seen to deliver relatively little tangible value. This situation is hardly surprising. Facebook didn't appear until 2004, followed by YouTube in 2005 and Twitter in 2006. Commercial television started in the UK in the mid-1950s, but almost sixty years later experts are still arguing about what makes television advertising effective and how to get the most out of a TV ad budget. During this 'trough of disillusionment' many of the specialist agencies, which have earned large amounts of money from selling social media technologies and tools, will face difficult times and the rejectors and cynics will enjoy reminding everyone that they always knew that social media was overhyped and irrelevant. The good news is that, if you subscribe to the Gartner model, our understanding of the true benefits and uses of social media will develop through 'the slope of enlightenment' to the 'plateau of productivity', during which time we will witness an evolution from the tactical gimmicks that characterize so much current activity, to game-changing applications.

DRAMATIZING INSTITUTIONAL WEAKNESSES

The principles that appear to determine the success of any social media initiative are becoming well established: be responsive, be human, be transparent. These happen to be the same, simple principles that underpin the performance of the most successful businesses, but unfortunately, most institutions struggle to live by them. They are slow, bureaucratic, faceless and opaque. They are not configured to work in real time, in terms of speed or resources, they are constrained by internal silos, distrustful of their people and remarkably thin-skinned when it comes to criticism.

Social media is no respecter of silos. I am amazed when I meet companies to discuss how they should manage their approach to social media, not by the number of people involved from different departments, but by the fact that most of them appear never to have met before. Equally, a simple question such as 'Who is responsible for tracking the customer journey through this organization?' is greeted with nervous smiles and finally the honest answer that, 'It doesn't really work like that here.' This was confirmed by a research study by the Chief Marketing Officer Council in the US, which highlighted that there is no single person taking responsibility for customer conversations across most organizations. Corporate affairs, customer services, IT and marketing all think that they own a piece of the action, but without anyone in overall control.[141] The rise of social media up the management agenda has highlighted how most institutions appear to have been structured to serve an internal agenda, rather than around the

---

[141] 'Giving Customer Voice More Volume', CMO Council Survey, 26 January 2009.

needs of their customers. To anyone looking in from the outside, their organizational model makes very little sense. Customers or other stakeholders don't know how companies are organized and, quite frankly, don't care. They expect to be able to talk to the right person at the right time, not lost in voicemail hell or fobbed-off with a poorly briefed junior in the customer complaints department.

This need to break down internal silos is not lost on Hewlett-Packard's Chief Marketing Officer, Mike Mendenhall: 'As marketers we have an opportunity and responsibility to drive change within our companies because all touchpoints now impact our brand and our revenue. Brands aren't defined by campaigns anymore but by the consumer ecosystem we nurture to support them.'[142] His company has recently re-engineered its European marketing function around an evolved role of the in-house PR team – which has been relabelled as an Influencer Marketing unit – and given control over social media, digital, measurement and sales, as well as the traditional PR role. HP was the pioneer of one of the few management ideas that has stood the test of time – MBWA, or Management by Wandering Around[143] – so its response to the rise of social media merits serious attention.

One of the key drivers for HP has been the need to respond faster to changing circumstances. In the typically pithy words of web commentator Jeff Jarvis, in the online world 'mobs form in a flash'.[144] Twitter has proved itself to be a particularly

---

[142] Mike Mendenhall speaking at the ANA Annual Conference, October 2008.

[143] Also known as Management by Walking Around, the expression was originally used by HP's David Packard and subsequently brought to wider attention by Tom Peters.

[144] www.buzzmachine.com, 16 May 2008.

effective disseminator of news and particularly gossip. A story can be picked up, tweeted, retweeted and then start trending on Twitter within minutes, which is the reason why it has attracted the attention of governments and security services looking for a fast way to disseminate public information. Unfortunately, compared to the hyper-speed of social media communication, most institutions are tortuously slow, weighed down by layers of bureaucracy, management cultures that don't trust people to make decisions, pedantic legal advisers and self-serving control freaks in their public relations departments. You still have companies refusing to put an email address on their website because they can't deal with inbound email or because the customer complaints department knocks off at 4 p.m. Expecting these businesses to be able to respond in real time to a tweet or a comment on Facebook is, at the moment, completely unrealistic. Equally, you still have companies taking five days to approve a corporate press statement, so to allow their employees to take part in a real time, unscripted and unedited conversation with customers online is going to require a huge cultural shift in the way that they work. Until institutional time gets closer to real time, this problem will not come close to being solved.

At the heart of most tortuous approval processes invariably sits a corporate lawyer. The legal profession has a problem with social media. It is completely counter-cultural. Legal arguments are based on slow and careful deliberation, so it is hardly surprising that the legal community struggles to come to terms with the anarchic world of the internet, in which unattributable rumours can go global within seconds and the traditional legal safeguards no longer seem to apply. According to Mark Stephens, a high-profile media lawyer with the firm Stephens Innocent, the legal profession 'can't cope with changes in technology'.[145] It requires a reappraisal of some of the fundamental parts of the legal framework, especially the protection of intellectual property and the definition of what constitutes free speech. An interesting test case has recently gone through the US courts about whether social media should be governed by the same libel laws as conventional media and conversely whether electronic conversations between private individuals, even if they are conducted in public, are protected by the right of free speech. Chicago resident Amanda Bonnen sent a tweet to friends, criticizing her landlords, Horizon Realty Group, which she followed up with a lawsuit. The company responded by suing Bonnen for libel after unearthing the offending tweet during a due diligence search, earning it the description, by one newspaper, as 'the dumbest company on earth'. Bonnen then made a counter-claim that her tweet should be covered by the same rights of free speech that protect private conversations between individuals. Predictably the US lawyers and media have had a field day with this issue, dragging up historical Supreme Court rulings and questioning whether traditional libel laws can be applied to the world of social media. Horizon, despite some furious back-tracking in the media, has discovered like most businesses that suing your customers is not the best way to protect your corporate reputation. The lawsuit was dismissed after a judge determined that the actions did not meet the definition of libel.

In another example of how the law struggles in this new world, the Southeastern Conference (SEC), one of the leading US college football divisions, in an attempt to protect the integrity of its valuable media rights, tried to ban its fans from sharing material captured during games on social media sites.

---

[145] Quoted in *The Times*, 2 September 2010.

Fans were informed that they could not 'produce or disseminate (or aid in producing or disseminating) any material or information about the event, including, but not limited to, any account, description, picture, video, audio, reproduction or other information concerning the event',[146] so even sending a description of the match or sharing a photo taken during the game was deemed to be a breach of intellectual property. Not surprisingly, this heavy-handed approach met with howls of protest and the SEC was forced to rapidly reverse its policy, adopting the much more appropriate line that 'personal messages and updates of scores or other brief descriptions of the competition throughout the Event are acceptable'. Charles Bloom, the SEC's Associate Commissioner of Media Relations, was disarmingly honest when he admitted that, 'We probably took traditional media rights language and tried to apply it in a new media world.'[147]

CONNECTING REAL PEOPLE

At its simplest, an effective social media programme connects real people on the inside of a corporation with real people on the outside. This ability to connect people is far more important than the actual technology that is used. If the social media fraternity has one collective weakness, it is in its unequivocal love of technology, often for technology's sake. They can't stop themselves drooling at the latest product to come off the Apple production line or the latest Facebook app. They would do well to listen to author and academic Clay Shirky, one of

---

[146] SEC policy announcement, August 2009.
[147] Quoted on PMA Link, 26 August 2009.

the leading commentators on the impact of social media, who has said that, 'Tools don't get socially interesting until they get technologically boring.'[148]

Success in social media is more dependent on an understanding of human behaviour than an understanding of technology. This explains why some of the best thinking on the subject is coming from anthropologists and social psychologists, who have an appreciation of the social and cultural impact of this new technology. Michael Wesch, an anthropologist, who runs the Digital Ethnography Unit at Kansas State University, is typical of this new group of leading-edge thinkers. This 21st-century version of Marshall McLuhan (and his army of willing students) is working on a number of projects that explore the impact of digital media (and YouTube in particular) on culture and behaviour, trying to answer questions such as what is driving our participatory culture? How do you explain the cult of narcissism and the spirit of the confessional that encourages people to share their personal lives and views with complete strangers on YouTube? What is driving people's search for deeper, more meaningful connections? How are relationships changing? Wesch is an unashamed enthusiast for the potential of collective behaviour, creating 'new forms of empowerment and types of community that we have never seen before'.[149]

Thomas Gensemer has been labelled Obama's digital guru. His agency, Blue State Digital, managed Obama's online campaign. During a visit to London in the build-up to the UK

[148] Clay Shirky, *Here Comes Everybody: The power of organizing without organizations*, Allen Lane, 2008.
[149] Michael Wesch, 'An anthropological introduction to YouTube', speech at Library of Congress, 23 June 2008.

election, he gave an important reminder to everyone involved in political campaigning that online marketing (like any other form of marketing) is first and foremost about relationships, rather than technology: 'What people want is an authentic relationship that just happens to be online . . . I challenge my clients, if this room was full of 100 people, forget about technology, what would you ask them to do and if you can't answer that question your problem is not technology. People have been bamboozled with the technology for too long . . . The real questions are "What are your goals and how can you use technology to achieve them?"'[150]

The Obama campaign has often been described as a victory built on social media, whereas in fact it was a victory for smart marketing. Obama started his political career as a grassroots community activist in Chicago. He and his team understood how to mobilize people and, most importantly, recognized that the trick with all campaigns is to turn engagement into action. During the 2008 presidential race, not only did they engage people with Obama's powerful rhetoric, but they also made it easy for people to become directly involved in the campaign by manning phone lines, canvassing door-to-door and donating money in their millions. Obama's phone bank system, in which visitors to his website could volunteer to call people in other states, resulted in a staggering two million calls just prior to the primaries in Ohio, Texas, Vermont and Rhode Island. Social media technologies helped to facilitate this action, but they would have achieved little without an overarching marketing strategy.

This point was reinforced by another member of the Blue State Digital team, Matthew McGregor, who heads the

---

[150] Interview with *Guardian* Online, February 2009.

agency's London office. McGregor has been involved in election campaigns for John Cruddas and Ken Livingstone and also in co-ordinating online campaigns against the British National Party. In an *Observer* article, ironically entitled, 'How the 2010 election will be won by blogs and tweets', he said, 'Blogs and politicians twittering get most attention, but under the radar a new form of organising supporters is happening. By energising people, and then giving them the tools to get involved and become advocates for the party, thousands of people are talking to volunteers, passionate about the issues and ready for a conversation. It is a new way of doing traditional politics.'[151] Organizations don't need a social media strategy, they need a smart marketing or communications strategy, with social media at its heart.

It is all too easy to compare the Obama team's use of social media – as a mechanism for turning engagement into action – with the unfortunately clumsy efforts of the Brown administration during the final months of New Labour. Brown continually struggled to shake off the 'analogue politician' moniker given to him by David Cameron. For all his intellectual rigour, Brown is not a natural communicator – Tony Blair famously described his skills in his memoirs as 'analytical intelligence, absolutely. Emotional intelligence, zero'[152] – and despite surrounding himself with some smart new media thinkers, during his time in office he continued to look uncomfortable in the chaotic, antagonistic and non-deferential world of the internet. His discomfort reached new levels after a disastrous appearance on YouTube. His campaign team – some

---

[151] *Observer*, 3 January 2010.
[152] Tony Blair, *A Journey*, Hutchinson, 2010.

have blamed his wife Sarah – must have suggested that it was about time Gordon embraced the digital world. Making a direct appeal to the electorate – without having to communicate via an increasingly hostile media – would also give him an opportunity to present his point of view. Unfortunately, Brown's awkward performance and particularly his smile – described by commentators as 'the death-grin' and even by his colleague John Prescott as 'the worst bloody smile in the world' – made his appearance on YouTube all too easy to mock and parody.

The Brown team compounded the problem by preventing YouTube viewers from adding their comments to the film, which simply gave the impression that he wasn't interested in the views of the general public. For a man fighting for his political future, this wasn't a particularly clever move and the comment from one of his team that 'moderating offensive comments would be too arduous' was unacceptable for a team desperate to engage the electorate in a grown-up debate about real issues. The other major problem in using YouTube was that the viewing figures were available for all to see. Brown's official Downing Street video attracted fewer than 100,000 views, whereas material featuring Brown picking his nose or struggling to cope during Prime Minister's Questions (invari-ably captured by right-wing blogger Guido Fawkes) attracted viewing figures in the hundreds of thousands. All this did was to simply dramatize Brown's unpopularity. There was no strategic rationale to justify this initiative. It was simply enough to be online, irrespective of whether it would actually help his campaign. The Brown team was guilty, like so many businesses, of putting the technology before the strategy.

SHOWING A HUMAN FACE

Brown was trying to show his more human side. Those close to the former prime minister speak warmly about his charm and humour and express surprise that he struggles to convey this to the public. It is a problem shared by many institutions. Showing a human face sounds deceptively simple, but in practice most corporations impose a bewildering range of barriers to constrain any genuine dialogue between real people on the inside and the outside of the organization. They create tortuous approval processes for all external communication. They restrict the number of people allowed to speak on behalf of the organization and try to control all dialogue through the imposition of formal rules and procedures. They look aghast when you describe how a forward-thinking business such as Sun Microsystems allows over 6,000 of its employees, none of whom have been formally trained, to blog on behalf of the company.

The US-based electronics retailer Best Buy provides a perfect case study for how to use social media to humanize an organization. Like all retailers, especially those selling occasionally unpredictable electronics products, it has to deal with a large number of customer service issues. And like all retailers, it finds that the phone-based way of dealing with problems tends to be inefficient and expensive: the phone doesn't get answered or when it does, you can't speak to the right person. Best Buy's advertising agency Crispin, Porter + Bogusky came up with a social media-enabled solution to this common problem. It created the Twelpforce – a Twitter-based service, manned by Best Buy staff, who respond in real time and as real people to any customer service issues mentioned on Twitter. It doesn't simply involve the customer relations department: more than 2,000 Best Buy employees are given the opportunity to share their knowledge and expertise – which is immensely flattering for them – and, importantly, represents a major demonstration of senior management trust in the skills and integrity of its people. As is the case with most successful uses of social media, the behaviour of the Best Buy Twitterers isn't governed by rules, but by a set of informal guidelines that the company also publishes on its website. It advises its people that, 'the tone of the conversation has to be authentic and honest. Be conversational. Be yourself. Show respect. Expect respect.' And my favourite piece of advice, 'The goal is to help. Not be creepy.'[153]

Numerous research studies have shown that people trust regular employees, such as the Best Buy employees responding on Twitter, far more than the rarefied creatures occupying the c-suite. It might be a stretch to describe professional footballers as 'regular employees', but in the eyes of the fans, they are far more entitled to speak on behalf of their clubs than the faceless money men occupying the boardroom. So the decision by the marketing people at Manchester United, at the height of the protests against the club's US owners the Glazer family, to close down the Twitter accounts of their leading stars and insist that all communications with fans had to go through the official Man United website, was completely counter-productive. This was the reaction of a corporate communications team desperate to control the news agenda. But, at a time when the club needed to win the trust of its fans in the face of escalating protests against the Glazer family's ownership, closing down one of the few credible and trusted links between the club and its fan-base was not the cleverest of moves.

A few months later, the Man United communications team

---

[153] www.bestbuy.com

appeared to find itself once more in crisis-management mode, thanks to the players' willingness to embrace social media. During the build-up to the 2010/11 season, club captain Rio Ferdinand, an avid user of Twitter, issued a tweet that appeared to criticize the club's inactivity in the transfer market: 'I wonder What would you do in our position. Would u refrain from making acquisitions, try 2 make a profit or just try 2 make a difference . . .' Within a few minutes a follow-up tweet was issued in which Ferdinand said 'And that wasn't referring to my club!' To the *Guardian*'s columnist, Matt Scott, it was fairly obvious that Ferdinand had 'been collared by Manchester United's Twitter police'.[154]

The major sporting bodies in the US have arguably been far smarter in finding a balance between giving their star performers the opportunity to speak directly to their fans, while maintaining some degree of control over the reputation of their sports. The NFL, which has a reputation for embracing new media, has encouraged the use of social media, but banned players from using electronic devices during games and from using social media up to 90 minutes before a game and until after all post-match media commitments have been completed. This appears to be working pretty well, although one player, Cincinnati Bengals' Chad Ochocinco, was fined $25,000 for using his mobile to post messages before and during a pre-season game. After paying the fine, Ochocinco apologized to NFL Commissioner Roger Goodell, appropriately on Twitter, hopefully not during a game.

The communications team at Manchester United was simply following the approach adopted by most of the world's financial institutions during the past few years. In the face of a

---

[154] *Guardian*, Digger column, 21 July 2010.

complete collapse of consumer trust in the aftermath of the global banking crisis, their first instinct was to tighten up and close ranks. Every public announcement was scrutinized and reduced to its blandest form. 'When in doubt, don't say anything' became the internal mantra. Nobody outside the hallowed halls of the corporate office was allowed to speak in public. Even now, when TV news reporters are sent into the City of London looking for a quick, uncontroversial soundbite from City workers about the general state of the economy, they are told that their employers have banned them from saying anything. This merely adds to the perception of most financial institutions as shadowy, opaque and disconnected from the real world at a time when they need to rebuild public trust.

I have always found it strange that banks are typically reluctant to let their employees have a dialogue with customers online, when I can walk into a branch at any time and speak to a real person. I accept that an online conversation stays online for ever, but, by the same token, that conversation can at least be monitored, unlike my conversations with people in the branch. Fortunately, a few of the more enlightened financial institutions have put aside their irrational fear of online conversations and embraced the opportunity provided by social media to reconnect with their customers. The US bank Wells Fargo is a pioneer within the financial services sector for its use of social media to open up channels between staff and customers. The company started its first blog as far back as 2006 – which is ancient history in the annals of social media – and now allows hundreds of employees to use blogs to interact with their customers. It was also the first bank to have a presence on Facebook. Rather than close ranks in response to the near collapse of the global banking system and restrict communication with customers to a handful of approved spokespeople, the Wells Fargo management recognizes that during a crisis, over-communication rather than under-communication should be the guiding principle. In the words of the company's vice president of social media, Ed Perpening, 'There's a lot of worry out there. That means we have to stay close to our customers.'[155]

To take a UK example, First Direct, which has always tried to operate by a different set of rules to the norm within the banking sector, has embraced a similar spirit of openness and transparency. It was the first bank in the UK to create a website featuring live comments, sourced via social media, and attracted headlines when it chose to feature negative as well as positive customer feedback in its advertising. The level of customer sentiment on the company's website has remained relatively stable since the site was launched. Nathalie Cowan, First Direct's head of brand, has noted that, 'Quite often customers self-regulate. Someone might start a conversation and then someone will disagree. The talk might look like it's going down a negative path but then someone will say they've had a different experience.'[156] This has encouraged the company to avoid responding immediately to every critical comment, relying instead on the First Direct community to respond on its behalf. First Direct started out as a telephone-based banking service and has applied the simple logic that, having built its reputation through conversations and referrals from satisfied customers, its digital activity should be equally open and conversational. The collapse in public confidence in the financial sector, as a whole, encouraged First Direct to leverage the strength of existing customer relationships.

---

[155] *USA Today*, 15 May 2009.
[156] Quoted in *Marketing Week*, 3 August 2010.

DEVELOPING A THICKER SKIN

Unlike First Direct, most institutions are remarkably thin-skinned when it comes to criticism. All too often they want to use social media only on their own terms – a monologue with uncritical and largely passive supporters – rather than as a means of engaging with all stakeholders, including their critics. If you want to know, in contrast, what a thick-skinned institution sounds like, note the response of former Orange brand director, Justin Billingsley, to a group of the company's critics. Google 'Orange broadband' and pretty high up the rankings you will find the forum orangeproblems.co.uk. Rather than seeing this as a potential threat, Justin Billingsley argued that, 'We should realise this is a privilege. We can see what the problems are and if we solve it, thousands of people know about it.'[157]

I spoke at a corporate communications conference recently and was approached after my talk by a very senior corporate affairs professional, who told me, 'The problem, you see, is that my CEO and chairman don't like bad news. In fact, they see it as my job to keep bad news away from the boardroom table. So I can't really go up to them and suggest that we facilitate an open and transparent dialogue with our customers, that might result in critical comments appearing on the company website.' My first thought was 'get a backbone'. Denial would appear to be the order of the day in the board-room: pretend that everyone loves you and bury bad news under the carpet. This tendency was confirmed in a report by recruitment specialists Watson Helsby,[158] which studied the

---

[157] Quoted in *Marketing*, 18 November 2008.
[158] 'Digital Communications and Social Media – the challenges facing the PR industry', Watson Helsby report, 2010.

attitudes of corporate affairs directors to social media. It concluded that, 'Many [corporate communications professionals] are struggling to make sense of digital media and the disorder it has generated. For many it is more "thought in progress".' The report's findings also suggest that in the dreaded vernacular of government, the corporate affairs or corporate communications role within most major institutions is no longer fit for purpose. Predicated on the illusion of control – the idea that a corporate reputation can be protected by tight news management and the careful nurturing of a handful of key opinion formers – the role no longer bears scrutiny in the era of consumer empowerment.

The last 20 years has seen the elevation of the once humble in-house press officer to the powerful role of corporate affairs chief – the person responsible for polishing the corporate reputation, keeping the critics at bay and the stakeholders happy. They have done their job so well that far too many of their internal audiences – especially those occupying the c-suite – have bought in to the idea that the world around them can be controlled, critics silenced and crises managed. Unfortunately, in a world in which trust is at a premium, influence is dispersed and criticism is cheap, these masters (or mistresses) of corporate spin are struggling. Stories can no longer be buried with a quiet word to your mate on the city desk.

Many years ago I worked for a financial and corporate communications agency which used to go into client pitches with two boards. On one board was written the word 'friends' and on the other 'control'. The message was simple, compelling and, given the spectacular growth of the agency since that time, highly profitable: 'We are friends with the handful of people whose opinions matter most in the valuation of stock prices or forming of corporate reputations and we know how to control the messages that they receive and transmit.' Oh, how things have changed. Authority and expertise have been dispersed to the extent that analysts are no longer reliant on personal briefings and are picking up their information from the web, and opinion formers are just as likely to be obscure bloggers operating out of their bedrooms as professional journalists or eminent academics. And the CEO is starting to ask why sites critical of the company are starting to appear at the top of the Google rankings. You are paid a big salary to stop this type of stuff from appearing, or at least that's what you told them. Welcome to the new world of the public affairs or corporate communications director: chaotic, complicated and largely unspinnable. It requires a completely new set of skills, in which an understanding of social media, behavioural psychology and influencer marketing is far more important than a bulging contacts list on your BlackBerry. It is a world in which many of the people currently occupying the leading corporate affairs roles are going to struggle.

It would also appear that the corporate world can't cope with the informality of social media, with one respondent in the Watson Helsby study saying that, 'This [digital communications] is all about engaging with people's hearts rather than their minds. Corporates as a rule don't know how to approach emotions. In order to operate effectively in the digital space, you need to be able to engage online as an individual rather than as a corporation.' This is another reason why many institutions struggle to show their human side. The formal, polished and legally approved language used by corporate communicators rarely feels appropriate in the informal world of social media. Authentic communication is loose, unpolished and informal. This is also the reason why it is usually very easy to tell whether a blog post purporting to come from a CEO has actually been ghost-written by someone in the corporate communications team. This is why my advice to senior clients is that if they are going to get personally involved in social media, to write their own blogs or tweets, rather then get someone in the PR team to make them sound interesting.

SOCIAL MEDIA AND THE CEO AGENDA

When Fritz Henderson was appointed CEO of General Motors in early 2009, he was faced with an enormous 'to do' list, not least the need to manage a company going through one of the largest bankruptcies in US history. At a time when most business leaders would have concentrated on keeping their heads down, Henderson decided that reconnecting with GM's customers was probably his most important task. He made a public commitment to 'being closer and more available to consumers than ever before', which included the launch of a 'Tell Fritz' website, which provided his customers with the opportunity to 'share ideas and concerns' with the person at the top of the organization. Henderson had already proven to be an avid user of corporate blogs and social media to connect with customers and other stakeholders, although these involved a reasonably high level of corporate control. 'Tell Fritz' was a much riskier initiative, putting him in direct contact with real people (including the occasional lunatic) and forcing him to answer sometimes difficult questions, without the 'air cover' provided by the GM PR machine. Despite all of the pressures he faced, he committed to finding the time to review and respond to customers personally, rather than farming the job out to some GM minion. He also hosted weekly 'web chats' and went on the road to talk directly with customers.

This story has a somewhat amusing postscript. Henderson lasted only a few months at the top of GM and was forced out by his fellow board members following a disagreement over strategy. His irate daughter publicly criticized the decision on the company's own Facebook page. Her offending comments (including rude words and poor spelling) were quickly removed, although not before they had been picked up by sharp-eyed bloggers. Some commentators suggested that this episode highlighted the dangers for corporations of using social media. Personally, I think GM made a mistake removing the comments as its actions made it look petty and simply helped to attract further negative headlines.

There has been much debate about whether getting directly involved in social media represents a good use of senior management time. The benefits of receiving real-time customer feedback, about the issues that really matter to them, need to be weighed against the number of hours this can soak up in an already demanding schedule. The *Financial Times* journalist Lucy Kellaway is one of those who believe that senior managers risk becoming distracted by a willingness to respond to even the most mundane comments. She was particularly critical of the UK head of Starbucks, Darcy Willson-Rymer – who is generally regarded as one of the most Twitter-friendly bosses in the UK – for responding to customers' tweeted musings about the Starbuck's business. Kellaway wrote how Willson-Rymer responded to a tweet issued by comedian Armando Iannucci to his 80,000 followers, in which he brought their attention to 'the slight smell of lavatory you get as you enter' the stores. Willson-Rymer responded within minutes, leading Kellaway to suggest that far from representing best corporate practice, this showed 'how social networking is making management focus on the wrong things and boring everyone in the meantime'.[159] She describes the willingness to engage with hundreds of Twitter-using customers everyday as 'listening gone mad'.

Even if senior managers agree with Kellaway's point of view and refrain from becoming personally engaged with social media, this doesn't mean that they should abdicate all responsibility for it. Far too many are currently leaving decisions about the application of social media to relatively junior digital specialists within their businesses. In part this represents an understandable technophobia on the part of the forty- and fifty-somethings in the boardroom, but it is also indicative of a misunderstanding about what they are dealing with. For many managers, social media is simply another technological innovation, like the arrival of email or mobile web access, which can be left to the specialists, the digital natives in the scruffy T-shirts who occupy the strange world of the basement IT department. The standard senior management response is to create dedicated social media units and then think they can tick that particular agenda item off their to-do list. They made the same mistake during the early years of the internet – creating dedicated digital units that quickly went native and began pursuing their own narrow agenda. Restricting knowledge and expertise to a digital ghetto also gave other parts of their businesses the excuse not to embrace the digital opportunity, so that it is only now that we are finally beginning to see digital in its rightful place at the heart of every organization. Social media should be on every senior manager's agenda because it represents a powerful change agent, forcing institutions to address fundamental structural, operational and

---

[159] *Financial Times*, 5 September 2010.

cultural weaknesses. By abdicating responsibility, far too many leaders are missing the perfect opportunity it gives them to reform and revitalize their hitherto disconnected businesses and to personally lead the change agenda.

CHAPTER 3

THE END OF CERTAINTY

IN SUMMARIZING THIS first part of my argument, I will describe what I would characterize as the end of certainty – a collapse of faith in the tight, empirical, rational models that underpinned our financial system and approach to business and marketing – and how this is being replaced by a new wave of thinking in many of our financial institutions, business schools and political parties. It is typified by a growing interest in behavioural economics but it can also be seen in the way that many businesses are questioning the value of longer-term strategic planning.

All major recessions have tended to lead to a fundamental reappraisal of business practices and have proved to be incubators of new businesses and new business models. Ever since Thomas Edison founded General Electric (now GE) in the middle of the major recession of the mid-1870s, recessions have given birth to many of the world's pioneering corporations, from Hewlett-Packard (now HP) at the end of the 1930s to CNN and MTV in the 1980s. *BusinessWeek* commented: 'Recessions don't produce record numbers of new companies, but they do seem to mark a turning point in the formation of new businesses.'[160] The survivors of the recent recession are likely to recognize that they are facing a new set of challenges, for which their training and experience has left them largely unprepared. In the words of Marshall McLuhan, they are 'trying to do today's job with yesterday's tools and yesterday's concepts'.

---

[160] *BusinessWeek*, 13 February 2009.

3.1 THE WALLS COME TUMBLING DOWN

'*In their desire for mathematical order and elegant models, the economic establishment played down the role of bad behavior . . . And flat-out bursts of irrationality. The incredibly inaccurate efficient market theory was believed in totality by many of our financial leaders, and believed in part by almost all. It left our economic and government establishment sitting by confidently, even as a lethally dangerous combination of asset bubbles, lax controls, pernicious incentives and wickedly complicated instruments led to our current plight. "Surely, none of this could be happening in a rational, efficient world," they seemed to be thinking.*'

Jeremy Granthan, a respected market strategist with GMO, an institutional asset management company[161]

On 6 May 2010 a trillion dollars was wiped off the value of the US stock market and no one knows why. What became known as the 'flash crash' has been blamed on an inadvertent mistake by a clumsy trader – what is wonderfully described in the industry as 'fat finger trade' – deliberate market manipulation by a group of speculators aiming to achieve a short-term profit, or simply a technical glitch. Whatever the cause, the irrational, herd-like instincts of the financial traders took over, causing the single largest one-day fall in the history of the Dow Jones Industrial Average. Stock market prices quickly recovered, but this phantom crash demonstrated that, even after the changes imposed in the wake of the global banking crisis, the financial system at the heart of our global economy is driven by unpredictable and often irrational forces.

---

[161] Jeremy Granthan, letter to clients, quoted in the *New York Times*, 5 June 2009.

One of the few economists to predict the global financial crisis was Nassim Nicholas Taleb, author of the critically acclaimed books *Fooled by Randomness* and *The Black Swan*. Taleb argues that the global financial system is conditioned by a prevailing arrogance in its ability to control events and that the predictions and forecasts, in which it has so much faith, are based largely on spurious measurements. Rather than being built on sound rational and empirical principles, Taleb sees financial markets as innately random and unpredictable, covered by a veneer of stability. For him, 'Globalization creates interlocking fragility, while reducing volatility and giving the appearance of stability.' He also talks about how investment decisions are no more rational and predictable than gambling and consequently demand a less empirical approach: 'Probability is a liberal art; it is a child of skepticism, not a tool for people with calculators on their belts to satisfy their desire to produce fancy calculations and certainties.'[162]

The leading bankers were suffering from the collective illusion that the system they were operating was governed by rules and patterns. It is Taleb's contention that we all tend to see structure when it doesn't really exist, because this gives us the comforting illusion that life is predictable and controllable. The difference is that most of us don't bring the world economy to its knees when we get things wrong. Taleb also points to a culture of self-deception at the heart of the banking industry, which remains despite the hard lessons of the banking crisis. This view is shared by Justin Fox in his book *The Myth of the Rational Market*,[163] in which he asserts, 'Even now after the

---

[162] Nassim Nicholas Taleb, *The Black Swan: The impact of the highly improbable*, Penguin, 2008.
[163] Justin Fox, *The Myth of the Rational Market: A history of risk, reward, and delusion on Wall Street*, Harriman House Publishing, 2010.

crash, finance professors are finding it hard to abandon rational markets and embrace messiness.'

The global financial system was the ultimate expression of tight thinking – a system dominated by a group of control freaks, wedded to an absolute faith in the efficient market model and confident in its ability to control events and in the validity of its forecasts. They were – to coin a phrase used in Tom Wolfe's *Bonfire of the Vanities* – 'Masters of the Universe': masters of the data, masters of events, masters of the future, until that fateful day in September 2008 when the collapse of Lehman Brothers confirmed Taleb's worst fears about the innate weaknesses of the system. Larry McDonald witnessed the collapse of Lehman Brothers from the inside. The company's former vice chairman has written what many regard as the most insightful account of the Lehman story. In his book *A Colossal Failure of Common Sense*,[164] he describes how Dick Fuld, Lehman Brothers' chairman and chief executive, and the other people running the bank, were intolerant of dissent – 'they didn't just rule with an iron fist, they wore brass knuckles,' which meant that 'you got your head down and did your job, otherwise you lost both'.

Another former Lehman insider was Andrew Gowers, who, following a career in financial journalism, became head of corporate communications for the bank's London office. He labels Fuld as 'the textbook example of the "command-and-control CEO"' and colourfully describes the strange personality cult that was allowed to develop around him in which, 'Those closest to him slaved like courtiers to a medieval monarch, second-guessing his moods and predilections, fretting over

---

[164] *A Colossal Failure of Common Sense: The Incredible Inside Story of the Collapse of Lehman Brothers* by Larry McDonald and Patrick Robinson, Ebury Press, 2009.

minute details of his schedule down to the flower arrangements and insulating him from trouble – from almost anything he might not want to hear. His ferocity could be intimidating, his eyebrows beetling tight over his hard eyes, his brutally angular brow appearing to contort in rage ... Fuld had used this aggression to consolidate his reputation as the most successful chief executive in the banking business and one of the most respected corporate leaders in America. But the style also contained the seeds of disaster. It meant that nobody would or could challenge the boss if his judgment erred or if things started to go wrong.'[165]

Fuld – as befitting a man whose nickname was 'the gorilla'– had an overbearing leadership style that made him reluctant to accept any questioning of his methods. For others at the top of the financial pyramid, the fault appears to have been a naïve faith in the integrity of the system and the innate efficiency of financial markets, which was almost religious in its fervour and certainty. Economist and author of *Obliquity*, John Kay, makes an interesting comparison between the attitude of the leading financiers and that of Robert McNamara, US Defense Secretary during the Vietnam War. McNamara's background was in business – he was formerly President of the Ford Motor Company. He brought his strategic planning skills to the White House, introducing a more disciplined approach to planning and budgeting, but was accused by his many critics of managing the war in Vietnam from a purely statistical perspective. He was likened to a First World War general for what appeared to be his belief that, given the relatively small number of Viet Cong fighters, a war of attrition would ultimately prevail. According to Kay, McNamara became obsessed

---

[165] Writing in the *Sunday Times*, 14 December 2008.

'with quantification, however spurious the numbers'.[166] Business guru Tom Peters is equally scathing: '58,000 dead Americans. Mostly thanks to that paragon of analytics – Body Count Bob McNamara. War by misleading measurement = humiliating defeat.'[167] Many accused him of being a cold-blooded technocrat who regarded the escalating casualty figures as simply numbers on a balance sheet. When asked by his British opposite number, Denis Healey, how things were going in Vietnam, he apparently replied: 'Just fine. Next month we'll be dropping twice the tonnage of bombs we are dropping this month.'[168]

In the aftermath of the global financial crisis, many politicians and commentators have called for the imposition of tighter regulation to prevent what they perceive to have been irresponsible and, in some cases, fraudulent behaviour. They have called time on the era of laissez-faire capitalism and light-touch regulation instigated during the Reagan/Thatcher years and sustained by their successors. Others argue that the collapse of the system was more a case of people failing to adhere to the spirit of the law rather than its letter: a view with which I have some sympathy. In his recently published memoirs, *A Journey*, Tony Blair warns against the rush towards legislation and greater state control as the only way to respond to the weaknesses in the financial system: 'I think the single biggest danger with the financial crisis was the view that gripped a lot of progressive politicians [which is a thinly veiled criticism of Obama] that somehow the people were going to

---

[166] John Kay, *Obliquity: Why our goals are best pursued indirectly*, Profile Books, 2010.

[167] Tom Peters, *Re-imagine: Business excellence in a disruptive age*, Dorling Kindersley, 2003.

[168] Quoted in the *Daily Telegraph*, 6 July 2009.

want the state to come back in fashion.' Predictably, he remains an advocate of the Third Way approach he shared with Bill Clinton, being 'not in favour of either the big state or the minimal state'.[169]

Financial institutions, such as Lehman Brothers, were guilty of gaming the system and would probably have done so, whatever the legal framework. Paul Moxley, head of corporate governance and risk management at the Association of Chartered Certified Accountants, describes how Lehman Brothers 'was able to make assets disappear off its balance sheet, simply by picking and choosing which legal jurisdictions it got its legal opinions and accounting standards from. But Lehman never broke the rules . . . Every bank that failed in the crisis complied with corporate governance requirements'.[170] He also makes a simple but powerful argument in favour of a focus on business ethics, rather than simply on the tightening of regulations: 'while you can dodge a rule, you can't dodge a principle.' As we witnessed with the scandal over MPs' expenses in the UK, adhering to the spirit of the law is far more important than adhering to the letter. Rules and regulations will always be subject to interpretation, especially when you can afford a bunch of smart lawyers. The politicians may like to think that by imposing a tougher regulatory framework they will stop financial institutions from operating entirely in their own interests, rather than those of society in general – and they think it makes them look tough in the eyes of the electorate – but unless those institutions are willing to operate in a principled way, loopholes will continue to be exploited. A looser approach, relying on a stronger code of ethics at the heart of

---

[169] Tony Blair, *A Journey*, Hutchinson, 2010.
[170] Paul Moxley, article written for *City AM*, 27 May 2010.

the financial system, may fail to sate the voters' desire to punish the bankers, but it is likely to be far more effective as a regulator of behaviour than the imposition of yet more legislation.

A CRISIS OF ECONOMICS

The crisis in the global economy has been accompanied by a crisis in the field of economics itself. The majority of the leading practitioners of the so-called 'dismal science' failed to predict the onset or scale of the economic recession and many of their prized theories and sophisticated mathematical models were proved to be predicated on false assumptions and the illusion of certainty. The philosopher and author John Gray talks about 'the intellectual failure' of the economist community: 'Ignorant of history, including that of economics itself, most economists not only failed to forecast the crash, but, mesmerized by the spurious harmonies of their mathematical models, were blind to the mounting instability of the financial system and failed to grasp that an upheaval of the kind that is currently under way was even possible.'[171] Robert Johnson, director of the Institute for New Economic Thinking – a think-tank funded by financier George Soros to challenge conventional economic thinking and modelling – has called for 'a broader, interdisciplinary approach to economics, taking in history, psychology, natural science – to take in issues such as climate change – and even literature'.[172] In his book *How Markets Fail*,[173] the economics writer John Cassidy calls for the

---

[171] John Gray, *Observer*, 29 August 2010.

[172] *The Times*, 5 April 2010.

[173] John Cassidy, *How Markets Fail: The logic of economic calamities*, Penguin, 2010.

replacement of the free-market-oriented 'utopian economics' that has dominated academia and policy making for the past few decades, with 'reality-based economics'. This viewpoint is echoed by Richard Reeves, director of the think-tank Demos. He has suggested a future model of economics that is far more humble, far more willing to embrace real (rather than modelled) human behaviour: 'Economics will emerge from its own crisis with more humility and greater openness to a wider range of theories, approaches and sources of data. It will be less scientific and therefore more realistic; less certain and therefore more reliable.'[174]

Another economist to come through the financial crisis with her reputation intact is Noreena Hertz, a Fellow of the Judge Business School at the University of Cambridge, and author of *The Silent Takeover*. Bono's favourite economist – thanks to her work highlighting the need to cancel the financial debts owed by the world's poorest economies – is a high-profile campaigner for a more ethical form of capitalism. She has described the past few decades as being dominated by a faith in 'Gucci capitalism', which she characterizes as 'lacking in real values' and based on the notion that 'human beings are nothing more than rational utility maximisers'. She has called for 'a new form of capitalism to arise from the debris – co-op capitalism, with co-operation, collaboration and collective interest at its core'.[175] Hertz doesn't hold back in her criticism of her chosen profession of economics: 'Over the past 30 years, economics became a narrow field completely out of touch with reality . . . I don't believe you can reduce the world to a mathematical formula. I start with the world, assume it's complicated, and

---

[174] *Management Today*, June 2010.
[175] Noreena Hertz, *The Times*, 25 February 2009.

ask where can I get help from a whole range of disciplines.'[176] Her work draws on subjects as diverse as anthropology, physics, geopolitics and neurology in order to understand the world as it is, rather than as the economists and statisticians would like it to be.

The faith in the empirical rationality of people and markets is being challenged by an emerging interest in behavioural economics. This fuses basic economic theory with a range of disciplines, such as psychology, sociology and anthropology, in an attempt to make sense of the often irrational and idiosyncratic nature of human decision-making, whether that of the neurotic and herd-like characters occupying the trading room floor or of ordinary investors. Reeves says that 'the field of behavioural economics has shown that in real life, people act out of fear, laziness, habit or desire to be like others – in other words act like humans, not walking calculators'.[177] Other commentators have talked about the shattering of the myth of 'homo economicus'. Ideas such as 'social norms' – how we tend to copy the behaviour of those around us – or 'situationalism' – how the situation in which we find ourselves also shapes our behaviour – are being given serious attention by many of the world's leading economists, politicians and business leaders.

A classic example of the use of behavioural economics in the NHS was described by the *Spectator* magazine.[178] One of the biggest problems facing NHS managers is the amount of sick leave taken by staff, not all of which is genuine. In response, a number of NHS trusts have signed up to a service provided by a company called Firstcare, which provides

---

[176] Quoted in *Fast Company* magazine, 1 November 2009.
[177] *Management Today*, June 2010.
[178] *Spectator* magazine, 1 May 2010.

healthcare advice for employees. Instead of simply having to phone in sick by leaving a message with a usually compliant secretary who doesn't ask any questions, employees are instructed to call a phone line, manned by experienced medical professionals, who give advice over the phone. Not only does this discourage bogus sick days but it also appears to speed up the recovery of those people who are genuinely ill. The number of sick days recorded by the 17 NHS trusts which have used the Firstcare service has declined by 28 per cent. Given the fact that, according to the NHS Health and Well-being Review, 45,000 NHS employees call in sick every day,[179] this represents a huge financial saving, simply through understanding human psychology.

The high priests of behavioural economics are two University of Chicago professors, Richard Thaler and Cass Sunstein, whose book *Nudge*[180] enjoys pride of place on the shelves of the world's business and political leaders. Cameron and Obama are both acknowledged fans of the *Nudge* philosophy, which argues that small prompts or nudges can lead to dramatic changes in behaviour and that these are ultimately far more effective than regulations or rules. It relies on a sophisticated understanding of the frailties of human behaviour and the conditions that need to be created so that people make the right choices. Some of the case studies featured in *Nudge* are fairly trivial, such as how the accuracy of male users of the urinals at Amsterdam's Schiphol Airport was improved by etching a fly onto the porcelain. However, the authors' study

---

[179] The Final Report of the independent 'NHS Health & Well-being Review', published 23 November 2009.
[180] Richard H. Thaler and Cass R. Sunstein, *Nudge: Improving decisions about health, wealth, and happiness*, Yale University Press, 2008.

of how inertia tends to lead most of us to take the default option when faced with difficult choices, has provided the intellectual underpinning for government policies around the world, including a new generation of opt-out (rather than opt-in) mass pension schemes.

George Osborne, also a devotee of behavioural economics and social psychology, has enlisted the help of Thaler to help 'develop policies that will work in a post-bureaucratic age where Labour's clunking tax and regulation measures have all too often failed'.[181] Meanwhile, Thaler's co-author, Sunstein, heads the Obama administration's Office of Information and Regulatory Affairs. One of the initial policy ideas suggested by Osborne includes redesigning household energy bills so that householders can compare their energy usage with that of similar homes, which the behavioural economists believe will be a far more effective driver of behavioural change than the traditional energy efficiency messages. He has also talked about providing people with financial incentives to encourage recycling.

The RSA's Matthew Taylor makes a similar point about the need to understand the real triggers that motivate behaviour when talking about the importance of 'voluntary mobilization' as a force for social change. This is based on the principle of finding out what people like to do and then helping them do it better, rather than attempting to make them do something they don't want to do: 'The state is forever trying to get people to do things; lose weight, stop smoking, get trained, get fit, recycle, pay tax on time, etc. So we the citizens are overwhelmed with messages with the net effect that we feel put upon and somehow diminished. But instead of starting from what we are

---

[181] George Osborne writing in the *Guardian*, 14 July 2008.

not doing, why isn't Government better at latching on to our enthusiasms?'[182] This type of approach has been successfully adopted in the area of health and fitness. The organizations responsible for increasing levels of sports participation among teenage girls have recognized that they will be more successful if they tap into the girls' existing enthusiasm for music and dance, than simply trying to persuade them that it's cool to play netball, hockey or lacrosse. As a result, the UK dance industry, no doubt to the disgust of the traditional sports lobby, has been given substantial state funding to develop a dance-based fitness programme.

BLAMING THE BUSINESS SCHOOLS

After the bankers, politicians and economists, the next group in the firing line, when it comes to allocating blame for the global economic crisis, are the world's leading business schools. The market for MBAs has exploded over the past few decades, with thousands of business schools churning out graduates, armed with the latest theories and case studies. Over 500,000 people graduate with an MBA every year. The most common criticisms often levelled at these schools is their tendency to over-emphasize the rational or empirical drivers of commercial success and their reliance on academic theories that fail to translate to the real world. Richard Brown, managing partner of management consultancy Cognosis and a lecturer at Henley Business School, suggests that business schools are far too focused on left-brain, analytical thinking, whereas the most successful leaders in business rely far more on intuition,

---

[182] Matthew Taylor's blog, 15 January 2009.

creativity and emotional intelligence.[183] The author and business consultant Dan Pink has even suggested that businesses should start valuing a Master of Fine Arts (MFA) qualification as much as they do an MBA, because the type of right-brain thinking coming out of the leading design schools has the ability to give businesses a genuine competitive advantage. What has become know as 'design thinking' is beginning to be taken more seriously in business schools. At its simplest, this involves solving problems like a designer; combining sound observational and analytical skills with the ability to make intuitive leaps. Professor Roger Martin, Dean of the Rotman School of Management at the University of Toronto, is one of its strongest advocates, arguing that: 'In a global economy, elegant design is becoming a critical competitive advantage. Trouble is, most business folks don't think like designers.'[184] He is highly critical of the limitations of current business school teaching: 'We're telling students that the big bucks are made by administering linear improvements – getting better and better at doing essentially the same thing,' he says. 'But the real challenge lies in getting better and better at a different thing: devising clever solutions to wickedly difficult problems.'[185]

Martin describes how designers rely on abductive logic – what he calls 'the logic of what could be' – as well as the types of logic grounded in the scientific tradition: deductive and inductive. Deductive logic relies on the application of widely held rules or principles to prove a point, whereas inductive logic draws conclusions or new rules from a series

---

[183] Interview with author, 6 April 2010.
[184] Quoted in *Fast Company* magazine, 1 April 2005.
[185] Quoted in *Fast Company* magazine, 1 April 2005.

of observations or findings. The problem with both of these logic methods is that they are reliant on prior knowledge or information, but the whole point about genuine breakthrough ideas or products is 'that there is no rule or pool of past data to provide certainty.'[186] The standard IQ test used by most educational establishments also highlights the limitations of an approach focused purely on analytical or reductive thinking. The IQ test is designed to achieve a reliable and consistent outcome. You should be able to take the test as many times as you want and achieve the same result; in fact, the validity of the test would be completely undermined if it produced different results. To achieve this level of consistency required the creators of the IQ test to focus on a narrow range of variables that could be measured quantitatively. The problem comes when you try to link a person's IQ score with their ultimate performance. Studies have shown that a person's IQ only accounts for 30 per cent of a likely outcome, with the remaining 70 per cent based on other factors. A more reliable test of an individual's intelligence and capabilities would require a more complex model, with more variables and, most importantly, the use of judgement.

Abductive logic, which you might also describe as the intuitive leap of faith, is based on the belief that 'if you can't imagine it, you will never create it', which is the polar opposite of the oft-used management mantra, 'if you can't measure it, don't do it.' Martin adopts the almost heretical viewpoint – at least from the perspective of most business school teaching – that 'The future is about imagination, not measurement', which echoes Einstein's adage that 'imagination is more important than knowledge'. He also suggests that, 'To

---

[186] *BusinessWeek*, 25 January 2010.

imagine a future, one has to look beyond the measurable variables, beyond what can be proven with past data.'[187] He describes how this way of thinking is the driving force behind the transformation of Research in Motion (RIM) from a relatively obscure pager company to the manufacturers of the ubiquitous BlackBerry mobile device. He credits the company's founder and CEO, Mike Lazaridis, for 'encouraging people to explore big ideas and apparent paradoxes to push beyond what they can prove to be true in order to see what might be true'.[188]

A new spirit of critical thinking is also being encouraged in the leading business schools. The *New York Times* was in no doubt about the significance of this change: 'Learning how to think critically – how to imaginatively frame questions and consider multiple perspectives – has historically been associated with a liberal arts education, not a business school curriculum, so the change represents something of a tectonic shift for business school leaders.'[189] It is a view shared by Rob Dixon, dean of Durham Business School, who argues that: 'We cannot stop the whole world revering a particular theory that works in particular circumstances and then does not work when the circumstances change. What we can do is to encourage a spirit of critical enquiry and critical reflection. Then when our students leave they will be equipped with a critical perspective that allows them to ask, "Why are we doing this?"'[190]

One of the severest critics of the leading business schools is Philip Delves Broughton, a Harvard Business School MBA

---

[187] Writing in the *Harvard Business Review*, 19 January 2010.
[188] *BusinessWeek*, 25 January 2010.
[189] *New York Times*, 9 January 2010.
[190] Quoted in *The Times*, 3 February 2010.

and author of *What They Teach You at Harvard Business School*,[191] which lifts the lid on the strange culture that pervades one of the world's most famous business schools. As befits a former journalist – Delves Broughton was formerly Paris bureau chief for the *Daily Telegraph*, in which capacity he managed to get himself blacklisted for asking impertinent questions of former Prime Minister, Dominique de Villepin – his criticism of MBAs is wonderfully colourful: 'If Robespierre were to ascend from hell and seek out today's guillotine fodder, he might start with a list of those with three incriminating initials beside their names: MBA. The Masters of Business Administration, that swollen class of jargon-spewing, value-destroying financiers and consultants have done more than any other group of people to create the economic misery we find ourselves in.'[192] He goes on to point out that many of the people running the major financial institutions which brought the world to the brink of financial disaster, were Harvard Business School alumni and describes how, prior to the financial meltdown, the Royal Bank of Scotland's business strategy, under the leadership of the now discredited Fred Goodwin, was being celebrated as a case study of best corporate practice.

We are witnessing an unravelling of the most fundamental building blocks of the commercial world and a collapse of faith in tight, empirical, rational models and ways of thinking. The people at the heart of our global financial system have to come to terms with a climate that is less certain and less reassuringly empirical. The economists and statisticians have been reminded that their profession is as much an art as it is a

---

[191] Philip Delves Broughton, *What They Teach You at Harvard Business School: My two years inside the cauldron of capitalism*, Penguin, 2010.
[192] Writing in the *Sunday Times*, 1 March 2009.

science and begun to focus on real rather than modelled behaviour. And the business schools have stopped relying on oversimplistic, rational and linear case studies and started thinking about preparing the next generation of business leaders for the chaos and ambiguity of commercial life. Welcome to the real world.

3.2 THE END OF PLANNING?

'No battle plan ever survives contact with the enemy.'
Field Marshall Helmuth Karl Bernhard von Moltke

The war in Afghanistan has forced the British army to rethink the way that it plans its operations. The old model was to plan an operation in detail, almost as though the soldiers were actors following a script: 'First we go here and do that, then we do the other, then we come home.' This highly structured approach has proved to be ineffective in the chaos of Afghanistan. It has been replaced by a new model, which defines an intended outcome, and a loose plan for achieving it, but then relies on a pre-prepared set of rehearsed actions that can be deployed as the reality unfolds on the ground. So, if there is a roadside bomb on the way to the objective, there is a way to deal with that, and a back-up for what they do next. It is a far more flexible and pragmatic approach that puts more emphasis on the judgement of the people on the ground and their ability to respond to incidents in real time, rather than the skills of the planners and theoreticians at army HQ. It isn't entirely spontaneous – different scenarios are planned for and rehearsed – but it has resulted in a more agile military response.

Without wanting to trivialize events in Afghanistan, the same approach is also being deployed in the supermarket aisles where real-time planning, requiring store managers to respond to actual shifts in buyer behaviour, is replacing longer-term strategic thinking. One of the first things that Sir Stuart Rose did when he took over Marks & Spencer in 2004 was to empower his store managers to make more decisions about the choice of merchandise they would sell. Prior to Rose's arrival, a centralized planning culture within

M&S had dictated which products were to be sold in which stores, irrespective of local needs. Faced with a hostile takeover bid from Phillip Green and a weakening sales performance, Rose undertook a rapid internal review that highlighted how the company's drive for consistency had become what he described as a 'core rigidity'.[193] This structural problem made it too slow to respond to market conditions and fundamentally compromised its ability to tailor its store offer to specific local needs.

Consistency is critically important for any business, in the sense of providing a uniformly consistent customer experience, but can become a weakness if it requires a slavish adherence to a centrally defined notion of consistency that takes away the ability of people on the ground to think for themselves.

There are some who argue that all forms of long-term planning are a waste of time and effort and potentially counter-productive. Jason Fried and David Heinemeier Hansson work for a software company in Chicago, 37signals. They revel in challenging received business wisdom and are the epitome of what you might characterize as the freewheeling, new technology ethos. In their book *Rework: Change the Way you Work Forever*,[194] they question the validity of most business practices, from meetings to strategic planning: 'Plans let the past drive the future ... this is where we're going because that's where we said we were going ... Plans are inconsistent with improvisation. Working without a plan may seem scary. But blindly following a plan that has no relationship with

[193] www.ceo.com, 1 April 2009.
[194] Jason Fried and David Heinemeier Hansson, *Rework: Change the Way you Work Forever*, Crown Publishing, 2010.

reality is even scarier. Unless you're a fortune-teller, long-term business planning is a fantasy. There are just too many factors that are out of your hands: market conditions, competitors, customers, the economy, etc. Writing a plan makes you feel in control of things you can't actually control. Why don't we call plans what they really are: guesses.' This view isn't necessarily shared by others in the business community. In his review of *Rework*, restaurateur John Vincent pulled no punches: 'Now that [the assertion that planning is a waste of time] really is dumb. Maybe in a low risk software company you can just do it, but if, like a restaurant chain, you have capital expenditure, or you are moving a factory, you had better make sure you plan the move, the stock-build, the overtime, the working capital and service implications.'[195]

Like all good polemicists, Fried and Heinemeier Hansson were exaggerating for effect (and did a good job of winding up John Vincent in the process), but there is more than a grain of truth in their argument. Strategic planning and long-term forecasting can, all too often, become a pointless exercise, in which people spend endless hours labouring over templates and spreadsheets that no one will read and certainly not use. People find a strange comfort in the process of planning, translating a complex reality into neat soundbites and over-simplified charts that will look good in a PowerPoint presentation, but fail to reveal the true picture. Equally, strategic planning can give managers a false sense of their ability to control the future, as if by putting something in writing you can somehow mitigate its likely consequences. Richard Thaler and Cass Sunstein in *Nudge* talk about ' "the planning fallacy" – the systematic tendency towards unrealistic

---

[195] *Management Today*, March 2010.

optimism about the time it takes to complete projects'. And I thought this was simply called 'being a man'. Writing in *Management Today*, arch contrarian Alastair Dryburgh of Akenhurst Consultants described forecasting as 'an activity that is at best useless and at worst actually counterproductive . . . forecasting nourishes the dangerous delusion that we know what is going to happen'. His advice? 'Stop forecasting, embrace uncertainty, start managing',[196] which is a pretty good summary of the loose philosophy in action.

CORPORATE AGILITY

Richard Reeves and John Knell, authors of *The 80 Minute MBA*,[197] express a similar point of view, suggesting that an uncertain world places a premium on teams with 'the agility to retack, seize new opportunities and question received wisdom'. I like their use of the word 'agility' in this context. Loose businesses are innately agile: able to respond quickly, often in real time, to changing circumstances. This could be why many businesses are abandoning received wisdom in the importance of strategic planning and adopting a much more pragmatic or tactical approach. You could describe this as 'real-time planning', in which decisions are made on the hoof, in response to specific circumstances. John Kay, visiting professor of economics at the London School of Economics, has coined his own term for this phenomenon – 'Obliquity', which he defines as 'adapting and improvising as you go

---

[196] *Management Today*, January 2010.
[197] Richard Reeves and John Knell, *The 80 Minute MBA: Everything You'll Never Learn at Business School*, Headline 2009.

along'. In his book of the same name,[198] he says, 'Life is too complex and uncertain for us to be able to predict and follow the most direct perceived route to success. Our knowledge is always imperfect, and events are influenced by the unpredictability of other people and organizations. Instead, our objectives are best achieved by a more meandering approach that enables us to adapt our strategy to changing situations.' Kay contrasts this flexible, pragmatic approach to achieving one's goals with a rational, scientific approach to decision-making: 'We do not solve problems in the way that the concept of decision science implies, because we can't. It's because our objectives are typically imprecise and multi-faceted, and change as we progress towards them. Our decisions depend on the responses of others and on what we expect those responses to be. The world is complex, imperfectly known, and our knowledge of it is incomplete, and these things will remain true, however much we learn and however much we analyse the environment.'

I know senior executives who routinely spend nine months of the year on strategic planning and only three months on actually concentrating on their real business. Much of this reflects the multi-layered structures of most corporations, creating multiple tiers of bureaucracy, all of which feel the need to be involved in the approval of decisions and require the almost constant churning out of reports, updates and forecasts. This, in turn, requires an army of report writers, form fillers and document processors, few of whom add much in the way of real tangible value to the organization.

David Brain, head of the Edelman PR agency in EMEA

---

[198] John Kay, *Obliquity: Why our goals are best pursued indirectly*, Profile Books, 2010.

and my co-author of *Crowd Surfing*, talks about the advantages
his agency enjoys by not being part of a major marketing
services group – the company remains privately owned: 'We
save a huge amount of time, that can be invested in the things
that really matter to the business, because we don't have to fill
in endless reports and forecasts simply to satisfy the multiple
layers of corporate bureaucracy. The genius of Edelman is not
what we do, but what we don't have to do.'[199] Brain also points
to the strength of the creative culture in some of the PR
industry's smaller and remote markets as, in part, a reflection
of a less developed bureaucratic function: 'They have the
freedom to think and are largely left to get on with things,
rather than having to waste hours on corporate form-filling.'
This desire to avoid the burden of bureaucracy and short-term
accountability is also the reason, along with the availability of
alternative sources of cheap finance, why a number of formerly
listed companies have taken the decision to go private.

The amount of time and resources spent on forecasting and
strategic planning might be justified if it actually helped
businesses make the right decisions, but this is clearly not the
case. In a study by McKinsey, only 28 per cent of senior
managers said that the quality of strategic decisions in their
companies was 'good'.[200] It would appear that far too many
managers find comfort and reassurance in the act of filling in
the reports, templates and strategic plans, and don't really care
whether or not it achieves anything. The disciplines of
measurement and forecasting also help foster the illusion
amongst many of our business and political leaders that they

---

[199] Interview with author, 20 May 2010.
[200] 'Flaws in Strategic Decision-Making', McKinsey Global Survey, January 2009.

can control events, whereas all that tends to happen is that the strategic reports gather dust on executive shelves and companies are consistently blind-sided by the unforeseen and the unforeseeable. As Harold Macmillan allegedly remarked when asked what he most feared, 'Events, dear boy, events.'

A SPORTS LESSON

It was fascinating to observe the progress of Team Sky in this year's Tour de France. The expensively assembled team, under the leadership of Dave Brailsford, is following the template used by Brailsford to transform the performance of Britain's track cycling team from also-rans to the best in the world. His meticulous attention to detail and belief in 'the aggregation of marginal gains' (the idea that even small improvements to every facet of the team's preparation will ultimately make a difference to its performance) played a critical role in Britain's domination of the velodrome during the Beijing Olympics. Brailsford and the rest of his colleagues at Team Sky are using this same approach in a bid to win the ultimate prize in cycling, the Tour de France, by 2014. During the races, nothing is left to chance. The team use their own mattresses, pillows and duvets during their overnight hotel stops to prevent the riders suffering allergic reactions. Team briefings at the beginning of each race day take the form of PowerPoint presentations, rather than the informal discussions used by the other race teams. The team bus offers the ultimate in rider comfort, including a lighting system that can be adjusted to match the riders' mood. The drinks bottles handed out during the race have different electrolyte mixes for each rider because they sweat in different ways.

Even the team leaders admit that they are sometimes guilty of excessive analysis, but nothing will be compromised in the pursuit of excellence.

It would be fair to say that Team Sky's debut in the Tour did not go to plan. Despite the meticulous preparation and attention to detail, the team's riders struggled in what must be the world's most brutal sporting event. It would be unfair to criticize Brailsford and his team right at the start of their five-year mission to win the Tour – especially given his track record – but it will be interesting to observe whether a strategy that works perfectly in the highly controllable conditions of the velodrome can work equally well in the unpredictable environment of the Tour. In the velodrome there are relatively few factors beyond the control of the team directors, other than the performance of their rivals. On the road, however, the teams have to be able to cope with the unexpected – the spectacular crash, interference from spectators and sudden changes of climate. As well as being highly organized, it requires the riders to be able to improvise and respond to situations as they arise. The former international cricketer Ed Smith, in *What Sport Tells Us About Life*,[201] claims that, 'many of the most inspired sporting achievements, like great works of art or innovation, spring from parts of our personalities which resist rational analysis, let alone planning.' He compares the type of professionalism exhibited by Team Sky, which 'likes to think it is in control – that it has got a work ethic, a clear process and a precise system', with the 'childlike freedom and instinctiveness' of amateurism. He quotes Brazilian football manager Felipe Scolari, when he was still living off Brazil's success in the 2002 World Cup, rather than struggling at Chelsea: 'My

---

[201] Ed Smith, *What Sport Tells Us About Life*, Penguin, 2008.

priority is to ensure that players feel more amateur than professional . . . we have to revert to urging players to like the game, love it, do it with joy.'

Smith also challenges the central thesis of Michael Lewis's seminal *Moneyball*,[202] a study of the scientific methods used by Billy Beane and his Oakland A's baseball team to compete successfully with higher-spending rivals. Despite having one of the lowest budgets in the major league, the A's won more games over a four-year period than any other team. *Moneyball* has become the bible for those who believe in the application of rational decision-making to management, based on unimpeachable statistics. Smith, who is clearly a bit of a romantic when it comes to these things, appears relieved that early gains the A's made through the application of an unsentimental, scientific approach have not been sustained: 'maybe ultra-rationality has a downside . . . perhaps sport's human dimension, its romantic core, was being starved in Beane's purified realm of free-market values and statistical analysis.'

The speed of change in the hyper-connected digital media world has underlined the value in taking a more pragmatic and flexible approach to business planning. When social media platforms such as Twitter can become mainstream within months, a corporate business plan built around an18-month or two-year planning cycle is of no more value than one of Stalin's five-year plans. It is also instructive to observe the behaviour of the most successful entrepreneurs. Amar Bhidé of the Harvard Kennedy School of Government has conducted a long-term study of the 100 most successful entrepreneurial businesses in the US and has discovered that only 28 per cent

---

[202] Michael Lewis, *Moneyball: The art of winning an unfair game*, W.W. Norton & Co., 2004.

had written a full business plan and 41 per cent had no plan whatsoever. This contradicts received wisdom about the critical importance of a business plan in ensuring the success of any venture and the assumption that the best way to succeed is to define a clear set of objectives and provide a detailed explanation of how they will be achieved.

Strategic planning as a discipline is not redundant, if anything it has become even more important: it just needs to be faster, more flexible and pragmatic and far less confident in its predictions and assertions. It needs to be less wedded to the annual corporate calendar and more appropriate to the real world. In his book *Obliquity*, John Kay maintains that, 'The test of financial acumen is not to predict the future (because you can't), but to navigate successfully through soluble uncertainties.'[203] I would argue that this should be a guiding principle for everyone in business or politics, not simply those in the financial community. Embrace the mess and uncertainty and leave forecasting to the weathermen.

---

[203] John Kay, *Obliquity: Why our goals are best pursued indirectly*, Profile Books 2010.

3.3 BIG SOCIETY, TEA PARTIES & THE LOOSENING OF POLITICS

'The truth is people are fed up of feeling that Parliament is a powerless poodle, that politicians cannot change things, and that power is always being drained away from them. In so many areas of our lives, people have more power and control than they have ever had before. But when it comes to the things we ask from politics, there is a sense that the system is self-serving, not serving us. This all needs to change if we are truly going to restore trust in our political system.'

David Cameron[204]

We find ourselves at the end of 13 years of New Labour, once again revisiting the periodic debate about the relationship of the state to the individual, family and community. David Cameron has unveiled the Big Society as an alternative approach to achieving positive social change, replacing what he sees as 'the heavy hand of the state' with a loose coalition of public, private and third-sector interests. In Cameron's vision, the state plays an indirect role in affecting positive social outcomes. It becomes an enabler or facilitator of change, rather than a top-down director, in the hope that this will empower communities to make decisions and shape their own future. Cameron has recognized that this will involve a significant cultural change, where people 'don't always turn to officials, local authorities or central government for answers to the problems they face but instead feel both free and powerful enough to help themselves and their communities'.[205] His

---

[204] David Cameron writing in the *Daily Telegraph*, 4 February 2010.
[205] David Cameron speech at Big Society launch, 20 July 2010.

vision is to build 'a society where the leading force for progress is social responsibility' and has committed himself to an ambitious agenda that includes 'breaking state monopolies, allowing charities, social enterprises and companies to provide public services, devolving power down to neighbourhoods, making government more accountable'.[206] Plans already announced include the creation of a 'neighbourhood army' of 5,000 full-time, professional community organizers; a Big Society Bank, funded from unclaimed bank assets, and grants to provide finance for the eclectic mix of grassroots organizations that he hopes will herald a new era of community activism.

Cameron's Big Society idea is undoubtedly built on a looser, more informal idea of how to deliver effective public services, devolving power from the state to neighbourhood groups, voluntary organizations, philanthropists and community activists. Alice Thomson, writing in *The Times*, somewhat sarcastically described the Cameron vision as, 'one happy family . . . helping the elderly to cross the road, reading *The Gruffalo* at the local school, planting oaks in parks . . . a nation of volunteers who scrape the chewing gum from pavements, build extensions for their elderly parents and help out at school kitchens in their spare time.'[207]

Much of the thinking behind the Big Society has been based on the approach and philosophies of Saul Alinsky, a community activist whose work in American inner cities in the 1950s and 60s inspired a generation of community organizers including a young Barack Obama. It is interesting to think what the left-leaning Alinksy would have made of the appropriation of his ideas by a right-of-centre political party in the

---

[206] Speech quoted on www.conservatives.com, 31 March 2010.
[207] Alice Thomson, *The Times*, 14 June 2010.

UK, although it underlines Cameron's willingness to look beyond traditional party boundaries. Alinsky's most famous book, *Rules for Radicals*, reveals the thinking of someone grounded in the real world, as opposed to the often naïve world of the typical idealist: 'As an organizer I start where the world is, as it is, not as I would like it to be. That we accept the world as it is does not in any sense weaken our desire to change it into what we believe it should be – it is necessary to begin where the world is if we are going to change it to what we think it should be.'[208]

The Big Society is not without its critics. During the election campaign a senior Conservative minister is alleged to have described it as 'total bollocks' and other campaigners claimed that it was too complicated and vague to have any impact on the doorsteps. Boris Johnson, in a typically off-message moment, revealed his cynicism by joking that, 'We must tackle the scourge of obesity, or the big society as it is sometimes known.'[209] Many on the left have criticized it for simply being a cost-saving initiative dressed up by the former PR man, Cameron, as some grand social project. There are also inconsistencies between the declared drive towards the decentralization of power – the word 'local' was mentioned 19 times in Cameron's speech to launch the Big Society – and the government's highly centralized approach to education.

Other critics have suggested that the Cameron vision is far too optimistic in its assumption that people's sense of altruism or community spirit can fill the gap left by the state. David Aaronovitch, writing in *The Times*, suggests that 'when Mr Cameron invokes an anticipated horde of "forward-thinking,

---

[208] Saul Alinsky, *Rules for Radicals*, Vintage Books, 1989.
[209] Quoted in the *Guardian*, 21 July 2010.

entrepreneurial, community-minded people" to run something significantly more than a museum scheme, he imagines a nation that doesn't really exist.'[210] Camila Batmanghelidjh, the founder of the Kids Company charity and a high-profile adviser to the government on the needs of disadvantaged children, worries that the Big Society might simply be an excuse for the state to walk away from its responsibilities: 'The Big Society looks like a lovely hollow balloon at the moment. It worries me – it just means that the government will no longer pay.'[211] Peter Mandelson, the architect of New Labour, is not surprisingly cynical about what he labels as a 'marketing device', which 'under examination [is] . . . like sand disappearing through your fingertips'.[212] Personally I liked Hugh Dennis's quip on the TV show *Mock the Week*, when he questioned why a government apparently committed to choice, was only offering the Big Society in one size.[213]

Another early initiative from the newly formed Conservative/Liberal Democrat coalition was to invite the public to help shape legislative and budgetary policy through the power of social media. This led to the spectacle of a different senior member of the coalition launching a new consultative initiative on what appeared to be almost a daily basis: Nick Clegg's invitation to the public to provide their suggestions for which laws or regulations should be changed in the interests of creating 'a more open and less intrusive society'[214] was quickly followed by George Osborne launching

[210] *The Times*, 23 July 2010.
[211] *The Times*, 14 June 2010.
[212] Interview in *The Times*, 10 July 2010.
[213] BBC TV, *Mock the Week*, 24 July 2010.
[214] Speech at launch of coalition government's *Your Freedom* Initiative, 1 July 2010.

the Spending Challenge website, which was designed to create a forum for people to share and vote on ideas for saving money and improving public services. David Cameron then embarked on a mutual love-in with Facebook founder Mark Zuckerberg, publicly thanking him six times during an online video conference for allowing Facebook to be used as a free platform for public engagement. This resulted in the launch of a Spending Challenge microsite on Facebook's Democracy UK page, which had been set up during the 2010 general election campaign. Zuckerberg, not surprisingly, reacted positively to this ringing endorsement of the power of the social network he had created: 'It's really innovative to open up policy making and engage the public in this way to try and create more social change.'[215]

Whether you regard this soliciting of public suggestions for policies and spending priorities as a genuine attempt to engage the electorate and involve it in the political process or simply a superficial marketing ploy, probably depends on your level of faith in the integrity of politicians. It would almost certainly appeal to *Wikinomics* co-author Don Tapscott who imagines a world in which 'a citizen could search the globe to assemble "my government", the ultimate in customized, customer-centric services. Healthcare from the Netherlands, business incorporation in Malaysia'.[216] He would have been disap-pointed by the initial response of government departments, during the summer of 2010, to the coalition's attempts to crowdsource policy initiatives. Despite receiving 9,500 suggestions, it appeared that no government department

---

[215] Quote in government press statement, 9 July 2010.
[216] Don Tapscott and Anthony D. Williams, *Wikinomics: How mass collaboration changes everything*, Atlantic Books, 2007.

was willing to alter any of its policies. Most ignored the suggestions and simply restated their existing policies. The *Guardian* quoted Simon Burall, director of Involve, a group that specializes in advising bodies on consultation processes, who said, 'You have to give the government some credit for trying to do this, but badly designed consultations like this are worse than no consultations at all. They diminish trust and reduce the prospect that people will engage again. This is a dangerous problem for a government that is going to have to take people with them when they make very difficult decisions.'[217]

In addition to talking about a new form of collaborative politics, it would also appear that a new spirit of openness is being embraced by UK politicians. The coalition government talks about the arrival of a 'post-bureaucratic age' in which 'armchair auditors' will have the interest and (thanks to the internet) the ability to scrutinize all areas of government expenditure. Communities secretary Eric Pickles was accused by some members of his own party of 'disclosure vigilantism' for insisting that the Department of Communities and Local Government should publish, online, details of all items of expenditure over £500, although his stance was praised by former Labour minister Tom Watson, who said, 'Transparent budgeting is radical and has the potential to transform public sector accountability.'[218] Predictably, Pickles' initiative brought to public attention a huge number of headline-grabbing expense items, from massages and acupuncture for stressed government employees to trips to Blackpool Pleasure Beach. Those of a cynical disposition might suggest that this

---

[217] *Guardian*, 2 August 2010.
[218] Quoted in the *Guardian*, 13 August 2010.

high level of transparency was also intended to highlight what could be dismissed as a 'culture of excess' under the previous Labour administration.

As with many recent political initiatives in the UK, what Cameron described as the 'largest public engagement project ever launched by the British Government', closely followed a template created by Barack Obama. On his first day in office, President Obama signed the Memorandum on Transparency and Open Government, creating what he hoped would be 'a new era of open and accountable government, meant to bridge the gap between the American people and their government'. It included rules governing the work of lobbyists on behalf of special interest groups, websites that would allow the American public to track government expenditure and a commitment to use new technologies to empower the public. This was quickly followed by the Open Government Directive, which required federal agencies 'to take immediate, specific steps to achieve key milestones in transparency, participation, and collaboration'. Obama, with typical eloquence, described the thinking behind these initiatives: 'I firmly believe . . . that sunlight is the best disinfectant, and I know that restoring transparency is not only the surest way to achieve results, but also to earn back that trust in government without which we cannot deliver the changes the American people sent us here to make.'

Across the Atlantic, it isn't simply the party in power that is embracing new forms of political engagement. Obama's opponents on the right of the American political spectrum have formed their own loose alliance to marshal their forces against many of his policies. The Tea Party movement started in early 2009 as a largely spontaneous, grassroots protest against the government's $787 billion economic stimulus package and Obama's healthcare plans. Despite its name, it isn't really a political party, but more of an informal movement, without leadership, structure, coherent message or any real discipline. Writing in the *New Yorker*, Ben McGrath described how, 'The amateur nature of the operation was a matter of pride to all those who were taking an active interest, in many cases for the first time in their lives, in the cause of governance.'[219] In many ways it is similar in structure, if not in political philosphy, to the anti-globalization movement, which also embraces a broad range of (often extreme) causes and interests and operates without defined leadership or formal structure.

In the aftermath of John McCain's failure to beat Obama in the 2008 presidential election, the Tea Party network has become the rallying point for Obama's critics and for supporters of the traditional right-wing agenda of small government and low taxes. McCain's former running mate and Tea Party pin-up, Sarah Palin, has outlined the movement's aims in simple terms: 'The process may not always be pretty or perfect, but the message is loud and clear: We want a government worthy of the fine Americans that it serves . . . And we're going to keep spreading that message one convention, one town hall, one speech and one election at a time.'[220] Given the Tea Party's success in securing two Senate seats in the 2010 midterm elections and mobilizing popular demonstrations at a local and national level, it is a message that appears to be resonating with those on the right of American politics, although it threatens to drag the Republican Party even further away from the centre ground. A movement once dismissed by

---

[219] Ben McGrath, *New Yorker*, 1 February 2010.
[220] Sarah Palin blog post on Townhall.com, 1 February 2010.

House Speaker Nancy Pelosi as 'astroturf' because it wasn't a true grassroots movement[221] threatens to become the most potent force in US politics.

The Tea Party has inspired a liberal alternative, the Coffee Party, whose mission statement is 'Wake Up and Stand Up'. It shares the Tea Party's frustrations with the slow pace of change in the corridors of power within Washington, but without the Tea Party's visceral hatred of central government or its racist undertones. It has already recruited over 40,000 members on Facebook and is promising to stage its own rallies. *The Times'* political commentator Daniel Finkelstein sees parallels between the fragmentation of politics, as typified by the Tea Party, and that of mass media, in that they are both having to respond to changes brought about by the information revolution. He envisages a future for what he labels as 'open politics', which will be 'looser, much less whipped, and characterized by the impossibility of anyone cornering the political information and keeping it to themselves. There will be more referendums, public consultations, petitions and the like . . . things will be less organized and less efficient. It will be harder to govern and pass legislation'. And may even prove to be 'more corrupt'.[222] This echoes a point made earlier by the Future Foundation's Jim Murphy, who describes modern electorates as 'almost ungovernable'.[223]

The tight world of the traditional party machine demanded very little of the electorate. They simply had to turn out every few years to vote and then defer all decision-making powers to the elected officials. This new world of looser politics, whether

---

[221] Interview on ABC News, 28 February 2010.
[222] Daniel Finkelstein, *The Times*, 20 May 2009.
[223] Interview with author, 27 May 2010.

it is Cameron's Big Society or Tea and Coffee Parties in the US, demands a much more engaged public. The fact that the Big Society message struggled to make significant headway during the 2010 election campaign underlines the challenge of reframing the relationship between voters and elected officials. There is also the obvious risk that the people most likely to seize the opportunity given to them to shape policy and government priorities will be the extremists. As we have already witnessed with the attempts to involve the public in shaping government policies and decisions, this all too often provides a platform for unrepresentative, bizarre and undeniably extremist views, from both left and right, advocating such things as the legalization of cannabis, the removal of speed cameras and the public hanging of health and safety officers. Loose may be the right way to reignite enthusiasm in the political process, but it won't be easy, especially when it comes to engaging the stubbornly disengaged parts of society.

Consumer empowerment may be generally considered as a positive force for social and political progress – holding politicians to account, reviving local democracy, transferring authority from narrow elites to the general public, democratizing the creative process – but what about the disempowered: the people without access to the internet or the skills, confidence or willingness to take advantage of these new opportunities? Empowerment will only transform society if it finds a mass expression and reaches beyond the activists and the technologically engaged: the millions who aren't currently online aren't interested in social media and can't even be bothered to turn up at the voting booth, let alone help shape government policies. Amidst all the hype about social media, we must never forget that consumer empowerment is not evenly distributed across the population. Millions of people in the

UK have neither the means nor the interest in checking out the reputation of their local schools and hospitals online, rating the performance of their GPs or satisfying a long-suppressed creative urge by creating their own movie or soundtrack. Unless we find a way to empower the currently disempowered, the exciting future promised by consumer empowerment will never be realized. Even those members of the electorate with access to the latest social media technologies can be apathetic or indifferent to the world of politics. It is not that they are too stupid to understand political issues; they simply have better things to do with their time, whether that means listening to a political debate or getting involved in one of David Cameron's social projects.

It is far too early to judge whether the Big Society is simply a relatively meaningless soundbite or a bold redefinition of the relationship between the state and the communities that it serves; or whether the Tea Party movement can sweep Sarah Palin or another right-wing icon into the White House in 2012. But both are emblematic of the power of loose, less formal networks to reinvigorate communities, drive social change and shake up the political process. Politics has embraced the concept of looseness in response to a new set of social, cultural and economic challenges. At some stage the pendulum will probably swing back to a top-down, centralized model, in which the state feels it is best placed to resolve society's problems. Until that time, it looks as though loose thinking will be in the ascendancy.

CHAPTER 4

THE LOOSE ORGANIZATION

HAVING ANALYSED THE wide range of social, cultural, economic and political factors that are encouraging looser models of organizational behaviour and described the emergence of a looser approach at the heart of our political and economic establishment, in this part of the book I will examine the attributes of successfully loose commercial organizations. I will showcase a range of best practice, from relatively small companies embracing leading-edge technology, to major corporations dealing with complex market conditions and employing large workforces.

When I wrote my last book I had hoped to conclude with ten immutable laws for businesses seeking to embrace consumer empowerment, but in researching the subject it quickly became apparent than any such approach would be oversimplistic and, quite frankly, disingenuous. This is even more the case with this book. I have therefore tried to provide a set of principles and broad guidelines, illustrated with case studies from the worlds of business, politics and beyond.

In general terms, successfully loose organizations:

- Develop and nurture strong internal cultures built on a high level of mutual trust
- Believe in the critical importance of operating in an open and transparent way with all stakeholders
- Demonstrate a high level of operational agility, which allows them to plan and work in close to real time
- Are highly informal, embracing the mantra used in the software industry of 'living life in beta'
- Regard collaboration with all key stakeholders as a fundamental driver of commercial success
- Have a looser approach to the development and management of their most prized brand assets

These principles may not sound as strong or as comforting as laws or rules, but in the spirit of loose I would argue that they are far more appropriate to the chaotic, confusing and contentious world in which we live.

4.1 TRUST THE PEOPLE

'I can imagine that in the military or in law enforcement you need some sort of control-and-command structure, but elsewhere, if you trust people, they will do a good job.'

Ann Gillies, UK head of HR,
W. L. Gore & Associates[224]

Being manager of the England football team is often described as the most difficult job in the world. Getting the best out of the highly paid egos on the pitch is almost the least of the challenges, compared with dealing with the unrealistic expectations of supporters, a voracious media pack and the infighting between the various bodies that claim to run the sport in England. The management style deemed most appropriate to getting the best out of the players, like any discussion about leadership styles, tends to swing between the authoritarian and the laid-back. We therefore saw the laissez-faire philosophy of Steve McLaren and especially Sven-Göran Eriksson, who tended to treat their teams like grown-ups and believed them capable of self-discipline, personal responsibility and a degree of self-government, followed by the more authoritarian style of Fabio Capello, if the media is to be believed, seeks more of a parent/child relationship with the players. Capello was even rumoured to have banned butter and tomato ketchup from the players' dining tables and dictated when they were to have their afternoon naps. When asked for a description of his daily routine during the recent World Cup, England's underperforming star player, Wayne Rooney,

---

[224] Ann Gillies interview, *Personnel Today* magazine, 22 July 2008.

described a regimented schedule: 'Breakfast, train, lunch, bed, dinner, bed.'[225]

The Capello approach appeared to unravel during England's underwhelming World Cup campaign. His tough and disciplined regime had worked well during the qualifying matches, when the players were together for only a few days in the build-up to each game, but stretched out over a four-week period, the Capello 'boot-camp' style of man management became less effective. Stories of player unrest began to appear in the press and it would appear that Capello was forced to break one of his self-imposed rules by allowing the players a beer to unwind after one particularly poor performance. The failure of the England team to progress beyond the last sixteen of the tournament, when at least Eriksson managed to lead the team to two valiant quarter-final defeats, might indicate that the Swede's looser and more laid-back style of management was ultimately more effective.

The debate about different management or leadership styles dates back to ancient Greece, with the polar opposite positions taken by Plato and Aristotle. Plato would have been on the side of Capello. He believed in the need for authoritarian direction if anything of value was to be achieved, whereas Aristotle, like Eriksson, believed in man as a social animal who needed a sense of participation in his own destiny. This dichotomy about the drivers of human behaviour was re-expressed in the 1960s by Douglas McGregor, a professor at the MIT Sloan School of Management in his Theory X and Y.[226] Theory X was his shorthand for an authoritarian approach

---

[225] Wayne Rooney quoted during press interviews on 12 June 2010.
[226] The theory was originally proposed in his book, *The Human Side of Enterprise*, McGraw-Hill Professional, 2006.

which assumes, somewhat cynically, that most people are lazy, dislike work, are immature and need direction, if not coercion, whereas Theory Y reflects a democratic or participative style of management, based on the view that people have a psychological need to work, want achievement and responsibility and can be encouraged to grow and develop in the right environment.

McGregor was in no doubt about the merits of Theory Y and deficiencies of Theory X as a way of motivating people: 'the philosophy of management by direction and control – regardless of whether it is hard or soft – is inadequate to motivate because the human needs on which the approach relies are relatively unimportant motivators of behaviour in our society today. Direction and control are of limited value in motivating people whose important needs are social and egotist.'[227] With all the hyperbole about the rise of social media, it is all too easy to forget that the importance of people's social needs and behaviours was being debated by business theorists over 40 years ago. McGregor was not simply a theoretician. He also put his beliefs into practice with the design of a production facility for Procter & Gamble in Atlanta in the 1950s. Run according to the Theory Y system of non-hierarchical, self-managed, responsible teams, this facility was 30 per cent more productive than any other P&G plant, in fact so productive that the company kept it a trade secret for 40 years.

---

[227] Quoted in Carol Kennedy's *Guide to Management Gurus*, Random House Business, 2008.

GORE'S CULTURAL GLUE

McGregor's principles continue to find expression in the management and organizational philosophy espoused by W. L. Gore and Associates, the manufacturer of Gore-Tex, plus over a 1,000 other innovative products. Ever since its foundation by Bill Gore in 1958, the company – described by *Fast Company* magazine as 'the most innovative company in America' and regularly coming top in rankings of the best places to work – has adopted a flat, team-based structure – they call it a 'lattice structure'. This is supported by a corporate philosophy that encourages initiative and a focus on personal fulfilment. You won't find any organizational charts at Gore, any sense of hierarchy, job descriptions or prescribed chains of command. Decisions are made by those closest to a project, no one can be told what to do, bosses are described as 'sponsors' and teams largely self-organize around specific projects, typically without any pre-defined leadership. The leaders of these teams emerge almost organically, being chosen by their team members for 'demonstrating special knowledge, skill or experience that advances a business objective'.[228] You might imagine that Gore would be based in California, alongside all of the other new age business models, but this is a business based in a bunch of nondescript buildings near the Delaware-Maryland border.

Ann Gillies has the interesting challenge of heading the human resources function for W. L. Gore in the UK, which mirrors its US operation by rejecting a traditional hierarchy or formal job titles. True to the company's loose ethos, there aren't any HR policies and procedures. One of the practical

---

[228] W. L. Gore website.

benefits of this approach is that there is far less paperwork generated than in a typical HR department. It also means that the department operates with a much smaller headcount than the norm and allows the HR team to focus its time on helping people understand the Gore values and culture, rather than push paperwork around the office. In an interview with *Personnel Today* magazine, Gillies explains how decision-making works within Gore: 'We do need to make decisions here, we're not a hippy commune,' she insists. 'It's about making sure something is happening, but not taking control – you're not managing people, you're letting the team work out the how and then get on with it.'[229]

Bill Gore was a Theory Y man. He trusted people to do the right thing and believed in the power of a strong corporate culture. He wanted to create a non-hierarchical, non-bureaucratic, self-regulating business, without rules, built around self-managed, small teams. Scale seems to be a key factor in realizing his vision. No facility is allowed to have more than two hundred employees, known as 'associates' at Gore. The company adheres to one of the key principles of any institution that aspires to operate in a looser way: it focuses on the creation of a strong corporate culture, rather than the imposition of formal rules and procedures. Simon Caulkin, writing in the *Observer*, described how for Gore, 'Trust, peer pressure and the desire to invent great products . . . would be the glue holding the company together, rather than official procedures other companies rely on.'[230] This cultural glue appears to be strong enough to withstand even the toughest market conditions. Karen Stephenson, corporate anthropologist and

---

[229] Ann Gillies interview, *Personnel Today* magazine, 22 July 2008.
[230] Simon Caulkin, *Observer*, 2 November 2008.

author of *The Quantum Theory of Trust*,[231] makes a similar point when she talks about the important role that trust plays at the heart of every network. Stephenson is currently helping the US Defense Department to understand the internal workings of Al-Qaeda.

A cynic, or maybe simply a realist, might argue that the Gore loose model is fine for a business basking in the huge profits generated by a series of blockbuster products, but that once the pressure comes on, it will have to revert to a more disciplined approach. In fact, according to Caulkin, 'Counter-intuitively, the best governance, especially in troubled periods, is the absence of external rules: Gore would rather rely on fiercely motivated people who, having internalised true north, have no fear of challenging leaders to justify decisions, and leaders who know they can't rely on power or status to get themselves out of a fix.'[232] Caulkin's logic is that the first thing to go in a crisis in most institutions is trust, to be replaced by a culture of blame and self-interest, while any sense of collective responsibility is abandoned. The Gore model, built on a deep reservoir of trust, doesn't allow this to happen.

It is interesting to consider how much of the money spent by an institution on compliance or accountability reflects a lack of trust in its people. In his book *The Social Virtues and the Creation of Prosperity*,[233] Francis Fukuyama suggests that what he describes as 'high trust societies' enjoy enormous compet-itive advantages over ones that are dominated by mutual suspicion and therefore heavily reliant on tight, expensive and

[231] Karen Stephenson, *The Quantum Theory of Trust: Power, networks and the secret life of organizations*, Financial Times/Prentice Hall, 2008.
[232] Simon Caulkin, *Observer*, 2 November 2008.
[233] Francis Fukuyama, *The Social Virtues and the Creation of Prosperity*, Penguin Books, 1996.

slow regulatory structures. This is also the reason why companies that rely on rules and the scrutiny of an overbearing compliance function, and feel the need to involve the corporate lawyers in every decision, are invariably weaker and less profitable than those that rely instead on building and maintaining a strong corporate culture, based on a high level of mutual trust. Running a tight ship can be very expensive when taking into account the combined salaries of auditors, compliance officers and lawyers, but it is invariably an ineffective way of dealing with accountability. Conversely, institutions, such as W. L. Gore, with strong cultures, can succeed through apparent informality. Professor Rosabeth Moss Kanter of the Harvard Business School asserts, 'As they become internalized by employees, values and principles can substitute for more impersonal or coercive rules. They can serve as a control system against violations, excesses or veering off course.'[234]

ZAPPOS CREATES A LITTLE WEIRDNESS

Building a strong institutional culture is far from easy. It requires time, effort and inspirational leadership. Online retailer Zappos has become the poster child for a new generation of web-based businesses, thanks to what has been described as a 'near fanatical devotion to customer service'. It calls itself 'A service company that just happens to sell shoes, eyewear, handbags, watches and a bunch of other stuff',[235] which is pretty understated for a business that was included in

---

[234] Rosabeth Moss Kanter, *Ten Essentials for Getting Value from Values*, Harvard Business Review, 14 June 2010.
[235] http://www.slideshare.net/zappos/zappos-amazon-022510

Fortune magazine's 2009 list of the top 25 companies to work for and was sold to Amazon later that year for $1.2 billion. One of the secrets to Zappos' success is the quality of its customer-facing employees, who neither use scripts, nor are forced to keep their telephone calls with customers to a set time-limit. They can also, at their own discretion, send notes of apology or even flowers to customers who have had a bad sales experience, without having to go through the usual approval processes. This means that customers don't feel rushed and are instead left with the impression that nothing is too much effort for the Zappos team.

This is completely at odds with the tight way that call centres are typically managed, in which calls have to be processed in a set period of time, scripts cannot be deviated from and all decisions have to be referred to senior management. Zappos can operate in this loose way, not because it pays high salaries or bonuses – it doesn't – but because it spends far longer recruiting and training its customer service reps than any other similar operator, putting them through a four-week immersion in culture, core values and service at its Las Vegas headquarters. New recruits emerge from this training pro-gramme with a profound understanding of the company's way of doing business. Any recruit who doesn't like it is offered $2,000 if they quit – a golden goodbye rather than the typical golden handshake. Around 10 per cent of employees take the money and run.

The Zappos way of operating has become so popular that the company now offers seminars for other businesses on how to recreate its strong corporate culture. Tony Hsieh, the company's evangelical CEO, has even undertaken a bus tour of the US to deliver his message of the import-ance of corporate happiness and to promote his latest book on the subject.[236] He described his personal motivation: 'I get asked by a lot of people outside of Zappos why I'm still here, because so many entrepreneurs leave the company not long after an acquisition. One of the big reasons is because what we're doing isn't just about making Zappos customers, employees, and vendors happy. What we're doing is a lot more important. It's about starting a movement and changing the world by inspiring and helping other companies to focus more on culture, core values, customer experience, passion, and purpose – all without losing sight of financial goals. We're starting a movement.'[237]

As far as Hsieh is concerned, all of the key functions of a business, including the delivery of great customer service, will look after themselves if the culture is right. But he stresses the importance of making sure that these values are not too lofty or theoretical – the type of generic words all too often featured on plaques in company reception areas. One of my favourite Zappos values is to 'create fun and a little weirdness'. Hseih also emphasizes how corporate values need to be 'committable' in that everyone has to live by them. Ongoing performance evaluations at Zappos are based as much on the way an employee lives and breathes the company's values and culture as they are on their contribution to its bottom line.

Weirdness is also at the heart of another pioneering business, the San Francisco-based Method, which manufactures environmentally friendly, non-toxic cleaning products. 'Keep it weird' is Method's idiosyncratic corporate mission statement, which is certainly more interesting that the usual guff about

---

[236] Tony Hsieh, *Delivering Happiness: A path to profits, passion and purpose*, Business Plus, 2010.
[237] http://blogs.zappos.com/blogs/ceo-and-coo-blog

'maximizing shareholder value'. Eric Ryan, Method's co-founder and chief brand architect, describes how the company tries to live by its mission by 'keeping it human, keeping it real and keeping it different'.[238] Like Tony Hseih at Zappos, he claims that his senior team put as much work into nurturing the organization's culture as they do into the products that are being developed. This requires a careful recruitment strategy to ensure that they hire the right people and a commitment to creating an open, collaborative environment in which people are comfortable with new ideas.

PRET'S CULTURAL REVOLUTION

The UK-based business that probably comes closest to the Zappos way of operating is Pret a Manger. The business, credited with revolutionizing 'the lunchtime eating habits of millions of office workers',[239] has built a chain of 240 stores, generating sales of around £270 million a year, despite spending less than 1 per cent of its revenues on marketing. It has done so by building an incredibly strong internal culture, supported by a significant investment in staff training and development: the company boasts that it takes three months to train their vegetable choppers, so that they are 'super fast, super accurate and can spot a badly chopped vegetable at 500 paces'.[240] It is passionate about bridging the typical divide between people working on the shop floor and those in head office, claiming that 75 per cent of its managers started out as relatively lowly team members.

---

[238] Eric Ryan interviewed for Microsoft advertising campaign.
[239] *Daily Telegraph*, 24 February 2008.
[240] Pret Fact No. 64.

One of the things that characterizes Pret's approach to employee recruitment is its willingness to hire strong, sometimes challenging personalities. These people may, at times, be difficult to manage, but they make a huge contribution to the sandwich-buying customer's experience. Pret has also been smart enough to exploit London's attractiveness to foreign students. A significant number of the people working the tills and coffee machines and stacking the shelves in every Pret store are non-UK nationals, who have taken a break from their studies or careers as accountants or architects to improve their English, making them, in the words of one commentator, 'the world's most overqualified sandwich makers'. Pret may be a fast-food chain, but you never have a sense that the people serving you are bland, corporate automatons.

Another business not afraid to celebrate the personalities of its employees is Air New Zealand. In June 2009 the company picked up a tweet written by one of its passengers, Tim Benjamin, praising the quality of the experience of his flight from Heathrow to Los Angeles and in particular how the 'staff were allowed to have a personality'. This inspired the airline's advertising agency, Albion, to develop a creative campaign featuring the tagline 'Personality Allowed' and showcasing the personalities of real crew members. Southwest Airlines is another company willing to accommodate big personalities. One of its cabin crew, David Holmes, became a YouTube star in 2009, when a video of him rapping the safety demonstration to passengers on a flight to Oklahoma City appeared online. Holmes invited passengers to 'stomp' and 'clap' along with his performance. It isn't a coincidence that Air New Zealand and Southwest are invariably at the top of most rankings of people's favourite airlines.

Daniel Pink is an expert on workplace motivation. His

latest book, *Drive*,[241] which explores the nature of incentives, provides us with some of the answers for why the looser approaches adopted by Zappos, Method, Pret a Manger and Air New Zealand are so effective. Pink argues that people involved in creative or cognitive tasks – the type of work that is increasingly dominating post-industrial society – are not motivated by money but by three key drivers: autonomy, mastery and purpose. Autonomy in Pink's definition is 'the desire to be self-directed'; mastery, the desire to be 'good at something', and purpose, 'the desire to make a difference'. Giving employees creative autonomy requires a high level of trust, but it sends out an incredibly powerful message about management confidence in the self-discipline and creativity of the people who work for them.

One of the companies Pink most admires is an Australian software business called Atlassian, which, once a quarter, gives its developers 24 hours in which they can work on whatever they want. What Pink describes as 'pure undiluted autonomy' has been responsible for numerous product innovations and solutions. Atlassian provides a degree of structure to this initiative by insisting that the outcome from the day is shared with the rest of the company. It calls these FedEx Days, as the team has to deliver something overnight. Probably the first company to institutionalize this type of autonomy was Google, which famously encourages its engineers to spend one day a week working on side projects. The company's senior vice president of engineering and research, Alan Eustace, talks about its 70-20-10 rule: 'We spend 70 per cent on core products, 20 per cent on emerging areas and 10 per cent on "wild and

---

[241] Daniel Pink, *Drive: The surprising truth about what motivates us*, Riverhead, 2009.

crazy" ideas. Those are things we may not have a business model for, but may be important in the long run.'[242] The list of product innovations generated by this approach has included Google News, Gmail, Google Translate and Orkut.

Google revels in the idea of being a loose business, espousing a freewheeling, anything goes ethos, in which supervision is a dirty word and failure is almost encouraged. The company's attitude to the failure of its products is almost nonchalant. When the company announced the demise of Google Wave – a tool for real-time collaboration and document sharing – Google chief executive Eric Schmidt said, 'Remember, we celebrate our failures. This is a company where it's absolutely OK to try something that's very hard, have it not be successful, and take the learning from that.'[243] His views echo those of business guru Tom Peters, who says, 'We avoid failure at all costs and cling to ideals like "order" and "efficiency". But we must embrace failure, we must glory in the very murk and muck and mess that yield true innovation.'[244]

Google loves the idea of living in a state of chaos. It even hired McKinsey consultant Shona Brown, in part because she wrote the bible of organized chaos, *Competing on the Edge: Strategy as Structured Chaos.*[245] *Fortune* magazine described her as 'Google's chief chaos officer',[246] which has to be one of the more interesting job descriptions. She describes the Google approach as 'to determine precisely the amount of management

---

[242] Interview on xconomy.com, 16 December 2009.

[243] Google company announcement, 4 August 2010.

[244] Tom Peters, *Re-imagine: Business excellence in a disruptive age*, Dorling Kindersley, 2003.

[245] Shona Brown, *Competing on the Edge: Strategy as Structured Chaos*, Harvard Business School Press, 1998.

[246] Adam Lashinsky, *Fortune* magazine, 2 October 2006.

it needs – and then use a little bit less' and believes that 'the way to succeed in fast-paced, ambiguous situations is to avoid creating too much structure, but not to add too little either'.[247] This is a loose philosophy writ large – freedom within a framework.

THE ENVIRONMENTAL EFFECT

Organizational culture is also shaped by the environment in which people have to operate. The architect Simon Nicholson was fascinated by the way that environment influenced learning and creativity. During the 1970s he came up with the 'theory of loose parts', which he summarized as: 'In any environment, both the degree of inventiveness and creativity, and the possibility of discovery, are directly proportional to the number and kind of variable in it.'[248] In simple terms, he believed that we all have the potential to be creative, but that this creativity is empowered in a looser, unstructured environment and that conversely it is constrained by tight, highly structured, controlled processes and environments. His theory has been avidly taken up by many experts in childhood development, who have seen the way that children's imaginations and creativity is stimulated in less structured settings. Even something as simple as giving pre-school children loose materials to play with, whether Lego bricks or empty cardboard boxes, is enough to fire their imaginations and natural curiosity. This type of play is described as 'open ended' as it gives

---

[247] Adam Lashinsky, *Fortune* magazine, 2 October 2006.
[248] Simon Nicholson, 'Theory of loose parts', *Landscape Architecture Quarterly*, 61, 1971.

children the freedom to explore their own ideas, without any structure or direction. The creative possibilities are endless.

Nicholson's idea is too fundamental to restrict to children's play, important as that undoubtedly is. It also has significant implications for all institutions that aspire to encourage the creativity of their people. If we accept his theory that creativity will struggle to flourish in a highly structured, process-driven environment, how can companies embrace the concept of 'loose parts'?

I was involved in one of the pilot programmes for a new workshop technique that applies Nicholson's ideas to the workplace. Lego Serious Play uses Lego bricks to encourage creative thinking. It is underpinned by robust research about the way that the process of construction encourages our brains to function in different and more powerful ways. During the workshops, you literally construct physical metaphors of organizational problems or challenges. It sounds odd, and I have to confess that I started the workshop wondering why we were spending our time playing, when we should have been working, but very quickly the magic of Lego starts to take over and you find yourself using the bricks to explain different problems. The people behind the concept talk about turning boardrooms into constructive playgrounds and the sight of a normally strait-laced senior director getting excited by his latest Lego model makes a refreshing change from the usual dull board meeting. Businesses such as Nokia and Orange use Lego Serious Play as a creative tool for strategic planning and it is also becoming a popular learning aid in schools around the world.

CORE VALUES

Having a strong corporate culture doesn't make institutions immune from criticism, especially when they appear to compromise the core values that attracted people to them in the first place. Whole Foods founder John Mackey is a journalist's dream – a successful eco-warrior who pays himself a salary of £1 a year and gives away most of his earnings to charity. His Whole Foods business, although struggling to take hold in the UK, has been amazingly successful in the US among the left-leaning, Obama-supporting crowd. He has attracted a loyal army of passionate brand advocates, who endorse his belief in the importance of locally sourced, sustainably farmed, organic produce, primarily marketed through the use of PR and social media. The business had almost two million Twitter followers and over one million Facebook fans at the last count.

Unfortunately Mackay decided to become involved in the highly controversial healthcare debate in the US, criticizing Obama's efforts to introduce a government-run healthcare scheme. This inevitably outraged many of his core customers – the liberal-minded, who don't mind paying high prices for Whole Foods products. They regarded Mackay's views as a betrayal of the Whole Foods philosophy and values. In the words of one customer, 'Whole Foods is expensive but people shop here because they identify with the social conscience of the company – now it turns out that ethos was just a marketing exercise.' Another commented, 'There are a lot of people out there who really invested in the Whole Foods brand, emotionally and financially. We are feeling really betrayed.'

Mackay's personal story and declared values have always been a core part of the Whole Foods brand, so his claim that the views he expressed were his alone and that Whole Foods 'has no official position on the issue' was somewhat naive. Protest movements started, stores were picketed and boy-cotts threatened. Mackay had alienated his most important audience by venturing outside his core territory – food – and by appearing to contradict many of the central principles that attracted people to the brand in the first place. At a time when many Whole Foods customers were questioning whether they could afford to pay the company's premium prices, Mackay's actions came close to doing irreparable harm to the business. As Mackay discovered, trust can be a fragile commodity. The Edelman Trustbarometer[249] – referenced during the first part of this book – highlights how distrust or cynicism is most people's default setting when it comes to dealing with institutions. We may not take the adversarial line, wrongly attributed to Jeremy Paxman – 'Why is this lying bastard lying to me?' – but, especially within Western cultures, we tend to see this critical instinct as a good thing. It is up to businesses and other institutions to earn the right to our trust.

Trust the people: it's a deceptively simple idea, but surprisingly difficult to build into the heart of any institution. One of my first clients was a major high street retailer that had been through a difficult few years and come close to financial collapse on a number of occasions. Not surprisingly, employee morale had reached rock bottom. A new management team was brought in to revitalize the business. They discovered that one of the biggest holes in the company's finances was caused by the amount of stock that appeared to have gone missing. Some of it was accounted for by shoplifting, but the clear conclusion was that much of it had been stolen by staff. This

---

[249] http://www.edelman.co.uk/trustbarometer

is called 'retail shrinkage' in the trade and is estimated to cost British businesses £567 million a year.[250] Their solution was completely counter-intuitive. They redesigned the company uniform, to include pockets on the trousers and jackets. The previous management team had demanded a uniform without pockets to make it less easy for employees to steal the merchandise, which clearly hadn't worked. The simple act of allowing staff to have pockets on their uniforms – which made life a lot easier for them by allowing them to carry all of the personal items we all take for granted – sent out a powerful message that they trusted their employees. It played a significant role in reviving internal morale and the level of 'retail shrinkage' was substantially reduced.

Building a strong, trusting culture requires a commitment to smart recruitment and employee development and above all the determination to inculcate a shared set of values across the organization. It demands a willingness to ignore the instinct to tighten up and impose rules, regulations and compliance procedures. Get it right, like the people running Zappos, Method, Pret and Google, and the benefits are enormous. In the words of Jack Welch, the legendary former head of GE, 'If you pick the right people, give them the opportunity to spread their wings, you almost don't have to manage them.'[251]

---

[250] KPMG, Fraud Barometer, 2009.
[251] Quote from www.leadership.com/management

4.2 OPEN FOR BUSINESS

'Our aim is to be a truly open, accessible and transparent business so that we can rebuild trust, and drive customer loyalty. I firmly believe that customer loyalty cannot be bought with plastic points or discount vouchers, it has to be earned.'

Andy Bond, former chief executive, Asda[252]

'Democratic consumerism' might sound like the type of snappy slogan you see on the platform of political conferences or the latest soundbite from David Cameron's Big Society team. It is actually the driving thought behind a business initiative unveiled by one of the UK's largest grocers, Asda. According to Dominic Burch, head of corporate communications and new media at Asda, the 'democratic consumerism' initiative started out with the simple aim of trying to get across the company's story, beyond the simple price message that has always been the focus of Asda's external communication, and address, head-on, the criticism that low retail prices inevitably mean a poor deal for farmers, manufacturers and other people in the supply chain. He says, 'We wanted to shatter the mystique about our low pricing and particularly the idea that by charging only £2 for a chicken or £3 for a pair of jeans, we had to be exploiting farmers or the workers in third world factories. We also wanted to engage our customers and try to bring the culture and personality of our in-store experience to the online environment.' He also talks about how Wal-Mart, Asda's parent company, encourages its businesses to adopt the principle that 'pre-buttal is the new rebuttal'. Rather than hiding behind bland, defensive corporate

---

[252] http://your.asda.com, 1 October 2009.

statements and allowing their critics to set the agenda, the Asda team, encouraged by Wal-Mart, believes that the best way to protect its corporate reputation is to express its point of view well in advance, be willing to debate with and even challenge its critics and respond quickly to emerging issues.

The initial trigger for Asda's decision to fully embrace social media was a charity cycle ride undertaken by the company's former chief executive, Andy Bond. He made a video blog of his journey and the Asda communications team decided to use this as an excuse to feature more dynamic and interactive content on its corporate website. This has since been followed by a host of initiatives, such as Aisle Spy, a blog written by employees, a Pulse of the Nation panel, which gives the public the opportunity to voice its opinions, and dedicated YouTube channels offering customer advice. In its most overt commitment to transparency, the company has installed what are described as 'Clothing Cams' in two of its factories in Bangladesh, plus webcams at its head office in Leeds, a carrot-processing plant near Selby (Carrot Cam), and at an automated milking machine at a dairy unit in Lockerbie (Cow Cam). These are unlikely to be the most exciting pieces of TV you will ever see, but the principle of openness is worth celebrating. Asda is also planning to introduce a Bright Ideas online forum for members of the public to share their suggestions about products and services. Burch's advice to other businesses still pondering the merits of social media is wonderfully down to earth: 'In lieu of some grand strategy, go and do some stuff and learn from it, but don't expect to be given any extra resources. You need to find a way to build activities like responding to tweets or comments about our videos into the day job.'[253]

---

[253] Interview with author, 21 July 2010.

All too often, co-creation programmes, consumer panels or social media-enabled forums have simply been superficial gimmicks, designed to generate publicity, rather than reshape business strategy. But Asda's initiative is real and substantive. When Andy Bond talked about 'introducing policies that encourage customer participation and feedback in a bid to involve its customers in the decision-making process', he actually meant it. He was in no doubt about the extent to which cultural and behavioural changes, driven by his customers' adoption of the internet, left the company with no other option: 'As a business operating in this environment, you can't cheat, you can't spin, you can't hide. Within seconds, customers can compare notes, demolish price structures, destroy marketing strategies and tell the world to shop elsewhere.'[254]

Asda is serious about soliciting the opinions of what it terms 'friendly critics', rather than simply talking to 'people who think we are great', recognizing that it is only through an open and honest dialogue with its critics that the company can hope to address the trust deficit that affects every major institution: 'Events over the past year mean that faith in big businesses is lower than it's ever been – because people have stopped trusting what's going on behind closed doors. So, from today, there is no "behind the scenes" at Asda.'[255] When a mainstream business such as Asda starts preaching the virtues of openness, engagement and collaboration – and then acting on those principles – you know we are dealing with a truly significant business trend and not simply a social media-driven fad. Asda is, at heart, a hard-nosed northern-based grocer, operating in a highly competitive market. It makes decisions on a sound

---

[254] Quoted in *Marketing* magazine, 6 October 2009.
[255] http://your.asda.com, 1 October 2009.

commercial basis, although it also benefits from the experiences of its Wal-Mart parent. Wal-Mart has been something of a pioneer in the use of social media in the United States – not always successfully, it has made mistakes along the way – but it has become extremely adept at using these emerging channels to engage its customers and counter the often vicious criticism it receives from activist groups.

McDonald's is another business to have faced criticism from activist groups plus a highly vocal health lobby. It remains one of the best case studies I have come across of how a corporate reputation can be transformed through a deep-rooted commitment to openness. The business may not be universally loved, but its willingness to embrace debate with its critics – just so long as they abide by the principle of 'civil dialogue' – and its commitment to transparency when it comes to providing information about the nutritional value of its products, has, at the very least, earned it respect. It has recognized the value in creating platforms for customers and other key stakeholders to openly debate issues relating to its business. For example, its makeupyourownmind.co.uk website, which states that 'anyone can ask a question and get a straight answer', has received over 850,000 questions to date.[256] This type of initiative is still treated with suspicion by many businesses – why encourage people to publicly criticize your company? But the experience of McDonald's, and of other businesses that have created open discussion forums, is that being seen to embrace constructive criticism and responding to it in the right way can be hugely beneficial for corporate reputations. They have also seen how the discussions tend to

---

[256] Figures quoted in an interview with UK CEO Jill McDonald, Marketing Society blog, 13 September 2010.

be self-moderating, with supporters often defending the companies against their critics. Wal-Mart has been particularly effective at using forums to rally its supporters to defend the company. Research agency Forrester describes how the company is able to harness the 'millions of [customers'] voices to their advantage, to use them as a counterweight to their socially savvy detractors'.[257]

What you might describe as 'the McDonald's template' is being followed by other businesses within the fast food sector, in an attempt to counter inevitable criticism about food quality and product sourcing. The rapidly expanding Chipotle Mexican grill chain was actually funded by McDonald's for a number of years and although the two businesses have since decided to go their separate ways they share a commitment to the value of open dialogue and operational transparency. The Chipotle founder and CEO, Steve Ellis, talks about the importance of 'food with integrity', preferring to invest the company's money on higher-quality products, particularly naturally raised meat, rather than on conventional mass marketing. The company's suppliers – mainly small farmers specializing in low-intensity agriculture – are given pride of place on the company's marketing literature. The fact that Chipotle is the best-performing financial stock in its category, would suggest that a commitment to fresh, high-quality ingredients and total transparency when it comes to the provenance of its food, is a far more effective driver of business success than a glossy advertising campaign.

In *Crowd Surfing*, we explored the different attitudes to openness and transparency displayed by three technology giants: Dell, Microsoft and Apple. Dell has been on a much

---

[257] Josh Bernoff writing in the Forrester blog, 21 October 2008.

publicized journey, from 'Dell Hell' (in which its reputation was being savaged online by its customers) to a model of openness and collaboration. It wasn't the easiest of transitions – Michael Dell is by his own admission a 'control freak' – but his company remains a brilliant case study of a corporation loosening up in response to new patterns of customer behaviour and new expectations. We chose to look at Microsoft and Apple because they are diametrically opposed when it comes to their beliefs in the value of openness. The Microsoft business model relies on a high level of collaboration with developers outside the business who test and refine beta versions of the company's software: 95 per cent of its business comes from these external partners. The contrast with Apple's closed environment is stark. Steve Jobs and his senior team don't tolerate bloggers (either internal or external) and show little interest in creative collaboration with people outside the business – although there are signs that this is starting to change with its willingness to encourage external developers to create apps for the iPhone, albeit under pretty strict conditions. Apple also relies on a very old-fashioned model of top-down communication and tight news management, although this didn't stop the company facing the rare experience of negative press headlines for its clumsy handling of the iPhone4 antenna issue.

The chapter on Apple in *Crowd Surfing* was, without doubt, the most difficult part to write. How do you make sense of a company that is so successful, yet fails to follow any of the increasingly accepted principles of openness and collaboration? *Wired* magazine was pretty much on the money when it came up with the headline: 'How Apple got everything right by doing everything wrong'[258] After considerable deliberation we

---

[258] *Wired* magazine, 18 March 2008.

decided that it should be considered as an exception to the rule. This might have been something of a cop-out, but we received some support for this view from the *Sunday Times'* Bryan Appleyard, who wrote, in a review of a biography of Steve Jobs, that, 'Most of these (the lessons from Steve) are harmless, but "Be a despot" ("It's okay to be an asshole, as long as you're passionate about it") and "Don't listen to your customers" might well prove fatal in the wrong hands. In fact, I'm pretty sure that any company that wasn't run by Jobs pursuing these tips would be brought to its knees in a fortnight. Jobs' Apple is not a repeatable formula because Jobs' isn't.'[259] If you have a messianic figurehead like Jobs, a design genius in Jonathan Ive, complete control of the product value chain – what technology commentator John Naughton calls 'the toll gate through which everything flows'[260] – and are enjoying an unparalleled hit-rate when it comes to new product launches, you can adopt Apple's tight and hyper-controlled approach.

The technology industry as a whole does not appear to be following Apple's closed model. Alan Duncan, the UK marketing director of Sony PlayStation, describes how, 'Life used to be simple: you launched a product and let it go. Now we are in a brand dialogue with consumers, which has forced us to be much more open. Sony used to be a closed company. PlayStation relied on mystery and putting out coded messages, but that approach is out of date. It doesn't work any more. The audience wants to be part of the company. They are battering down the doors. It used to be about being clever and creating mystery around the brand, but credibility now is all

---

[259] Bryan Appleyard, *Sunday Times*, 22 March 2009.
[260] *Observer*, 26 September 2010.

about honesty.'[261] Sony has realized that its core customers demand a level of involvement and access to the inner workings of the business. They expect to be consulted on new product developments and given the opportunity to share and debate ideas, hence Sony's decision to create PlayStation Blog Share as a web forum for fans to share 'comments, critiques, questions and suggestions'.[262] This allows Sony console owners to submit one idea per day on a feature they would like to see. After it has been approved, other users of the forum can vote for their favourites, with the most popular ideas sent to the development teams within Sony. Even the senders of unworkable ideas are provided with an explanation of why their suggestions have not been considered.

Openness is not without limit. Organizations should avoid confusing a spirit of openness and transparency with the abdication of all control over sensitive or commercially valuable information. Stakeholders expect to know what type of business they are dealing with and demand an honest dialogue, but will accept that there will occasionally be constraints on what information can be made available to them. This is well illustrated by the experiences of a leading retail group, which in a spirit of transparency had decided that the part of their website used to share messages and debate issues with their staff would be accessible to people outside the company. What better way to demonstrate a corporate commitment to transparency? Unfortunately, they quickly realized that some of the most avid external observers of these staff discussions were journalists. A Monday morning rallying cry to staff about the need to improve sales after a disappointing weekend at

---

[261] *Marketing* magazine, 22 September 2009.
[262] http://share.blog.us.playstation.com/

the tills rapidly became a damaging media headline about 'company in crisis'. There are some things that are best left to the internal audience and this part of the website is now not accessible to those outside the company. This is not a betrayal of the principles of openness, but simply a recognition that there is a time and a place to communicate commercially sensitive information. The company has been open in its explanation of why it has made the change: if you can't be entirely open, at least be honest.

4.3 LIVING LIFE IN BETA

'It's not about the finished story, but about the ongoing story. It's a conversation. And since most conversations don't have a conclusion, they are ongoing. We live a life in beta.'

Bruce Nussbaum, assistant managing editor,
BusinessWeek [263]

TCHO, the San Francisco-based chocolatier, describes itself as 'where technology meets chocolate; where Silicon Valley start-up meets San Francisco food culture'.[264] It was founded by Louis Rossetto, the co-founder of *Wired* magazine, and Timothy Childs, whose portfolio includes developing visualization software for Nasa's Space Shuttle Project, so it is not surprising that it has chosen a business model more commonly found in the software industry than the traditional world of confectionery. *Wired* labelled it as 'the world's most technologically obsessed chocolate company' and described how it uses the latest technology to monitor growing conditions, manage the unpredictable fermentation process of the cocoa beans and develop new flavours.[265] In a carbon copy of the approach used by software manufacturers, TCHO hands out what it calls, 'beta editions' of its chocolate bars, in plain brown bags, to its regular customers on an almost daily basis. Software developers routinely issue prototypes or unfinished products, described as 'beta models', to the developer community in order to iron out bugs and identify potential new applications. Working in this way provides TCHO with extensive and

---

[263] 'Designers are the enemy of design', *BusinessWeek*, 18 March 2007.
[264] TCHO website.
[265] *Wired* magazine, 21 December 2009.

almost immediate customer feedback – from real people consuming the product in real environments and in close to real time – helping it to fine-tune its products, without the need to invest in expensive product testing research. It also flatters the egos of its most important customers, who think of themselves as co-creators or collaborators, rather than simply customers. They will forgive the occasional product that doesn't come up to scratch because they appreciate the opportunity that has been given to them to express their opinions and contribute to a collective endeavour.

This outsourcing of the product development process, using external collaborators, either experts or amateur enthusiasts, to complement or even replace internal specialists is known within the software industry as Open Innovation. One of the evangelists of this approach has been the writer Eric Raymond, who came up with the metaphor of the 'cathedral and the bazaar' to describe two very different models of innovation.[266] The bazaar represents the loose, open source approach, harnessing the skills of the wider developer community, whereas the 'cathedral' represents the traditional, tightly controlled model. Raymond argues that both approaches are valid and potentially complementary. The experience of the software industry suggests that the 'bazaar' is not particularly effective at originating concepts, which still rely on the spark of individual genius to make them happen, but is very effective at testing and improving them. So in the case of TCHO, you still need the chocolate experts, working within the company's 'cathedral', to come up with the original ideas, which can then be tested and fine-tuned by the members of the chocolate loving 'bazaar'.

---

[266] Eric Raymond, *The Cathedral & the Bazaar: Musings on Linux and open source by an accidental revolutionary*, Pragma, 2001.

Living life in a permanent state of beta requires a completely new way of thinking. Issuing your customers with something that is rough, incomplete and possibly even sub-standard seems counter-intuitive, but there is growing evidence that people don't necessarily want the perfect product or the glossy image of the company that appears in the brochure; they prefer to deal with something a bit ragged around the edges that they can adapt or improve. I was particularly taken by the merchand- izing strategy adopted by the Future Group in their Big Bazaar store in Mumbai. The company's research has shown that Indian consumers don't like orderly retail displays, preferring the untidy way that goods are sold in traditional bazaars and local corner shops. Future Group has responded by introducing a concept aptly described as 'organized chaos'. Cluttered displays and a general air of disorder has proved to be a huge success, despite the fact that the Big Bazaar was described by one commentator as 'looking as though it had been looted'. The design industry has even come up with the term 'messy vitality' to describe the kind of organized chaos – as opposed to sterile order – that characterizes the most dynamic and interesting urban spaces or shopping experiences. One of the reasons why farmers' markets have been so successful, apart from the quality of the produce, is because of the informal, somewhat amateurish way in which the products are displayed, which makes them feel more authentic.

The idea of 'messy vitality' is also beginning to be applied to the way that companies approach their marketing. Instead of issuing perfectly formed items of communication – such as a lavishly produced, multi-million-pound television commercial – some businesses are sending out deliberately half-finished or unpolished pieces of work. The author Clay Shirky believes that if something looks too perfect, consumers won't touch it, as 'it leaves no space for me'.[267] Innocent Foods – described by *The Times* as adopting a 'happy clappy approach to marketing' – even criticized one of its agencies for producing work that looked too professional. Innocent may have become a multi-million-pound global business, but its packaging and marketing materials remain as informal and understated as they were when the company was founded by three friends not long out of university. The *Guardian*'s political columnist Jonathan Freedland went so far as to suggest that the brand's marketing style was being copied by Gordon Brown's team during the 2010 election campaign: 'They've taken a look at the branding of Innocent smoothies, hoping the authentic, unspun look might fit their own "unairbrushable" product, G. Brown.'[268]

I recently had a conversation with the head of a UK charity who had just returned from seeing the relief efforts undertaken by his organization following the Haiti earthquake. He had taken his video camera with him so that he could show footage of the work that was being done on the island to his fellow board members back in London. A colleague suggested that this rough footage, accompanied by an unscripted commentary, should be sent to the charity's leading donors. Others argued that it was far too unprofessional and unpolished and needed to be properly edited if it was to be sent to such an important group of people. In the end they decided to send out the rough, unedited version. Their bravery was rewarded as, within days, the rough but authentic film generated a wave of cheques from donors.

Corporate communication is becoming increasingly informal.

---

[267] Clay Shirky, *Here Comes Everybody: The power of organizing without organizations*, Allen Lane, 2008.
[268] *Guardian*, 19 January 2010.

During British Airways' industrial dispute with the Unite trade union, Willie Walsh, the airline's chief executive, started posting a series of informal videos on YouTube and BA.com explaining the company's position and addressing customers' concerns. The videos were simple affairs, featuring a casually dressed Walsh talking in an informal tone about the airline's response to the strike. They were filmed and edited in a matter of hours, allowing BA to provide its customers and other stakeholders with almost a real-time update. A survey undertaken by *Marketing* magazine revealed that 19 per cent of those who had seen the videos had an enhanced view of the airline and more than three-quarters felt as supportive or more so than before. Chris Davies, BA's head of digital marketing, said, 'Although we will continue to use traditional channels, putting social media at the heart of our overall communication has allowed us to take a fleet of foot approach.'[269] This is why my advice to companies is to invest in a decent film camera and appoint someone as their official camera person/director. Their ability to capture rough but authentic and timely footage will more than compensate for its low production values. According to YouTube, video currently accounts for a third of web traffic and by 2013 it will be 90 per cent.[270] The future is video, which means that all institutions need to start thinking of themselves as film companies.

This reassessment of the importance of high production values, brought about by the idea of living life in a permanent state of beta, represents a particular challenge for the creative industry – designers, brand identity specialists and advertising

---

[269] *Marketing* magazine, 23 March 2010.
[270] Figures provided by Bruce Daisley, YouTube sales leader, 23 September 2010.

agencies – who have always argued that the creative process requires months of careful thought and craftsmanship. Convincing their clients that this was the only way to develop the best work clearly suited the agencies, as it allowed them to make a case for charging large amounts of billable time, while it wasn't a problem for most clients who were happy to concentrate their advertising investment on one or two major campaigns each year. Increasingly, this is no longer the case; few clients have the luxury or budgets to allow their agencies to spend months crafting and fine-tuning an expensive piece of film that will be shown a few times before disappearing into the archives.

As well as questioning the validity or necessity of high production values, the idea of living life in beta also redefines creativity as a continuous collaborative process, rather than an end in itself. Bruce Nussbaum is an assistant managing editor at *BusinessWeek*, responsible for the magazine's innovation and design coverage and has been named as one of the 40 most powerful people in the US design industry. He says, 'People want to be in the design sandbox, so you have to figure out a way to get them in and design with them.'[271] Stephen Bell, creative director at design agency Coley Porter Bell, talks about the need to 'build looseness into a design' to give people an opportunity to collaborate and customize, but within a defined structure: 'Why try to make things perfect and fixed in the knowledge that it is likely to be pulled apart?'[272]

The former head of UK marketing at Microsoft Advertising, Alex Marks, has even gone so far as to suggest that marketers

---

[271] Bruce Nussbaum, 'Designers are the enemy of design', *BusinessWeek*, 18 March 2007.
[272] Stephen Bell interview with author, 18 June 2010.

should allow their work to get 'messed up', which is an unusual objective given the reverence with which most businesses like to treat their creative output. I would propose that this be slightly modified and that companies should encourage customers to play with their brand communication. A simple illustration of this was provided by the creative team behind the relaunch of the Mini in the US. Instead of a conventional magazine ad, featuring a highly art-directed shot of the car, they provided magazine readers with a set of stickers that they could peel off and customize their own Mini photo.

Advertising in general is becoming less passive and more interactive. In an attempt to gain or retain people's attention, we are being encouraged to suggest new plot lines for television commercials, send digital content to digitally enabled billboards via Bluetooth or immerse ourselves in rich online experiences.

Robert Campbell is a prominent creative director who has worked with some of the largest advertising agency groups and crafted award-winning campaigns for clients such as Virgin and Marks & Spencer. Currently creative director at the appropriately named Beta, a recent start-up in the UK market, Campbell argues that the advertising industry has to move from what he describes as 'the pitching of perfection'[273] to a much looser, rougher style of work, in which the advertising industry has to stop focusing on the creation of one or two monolithic campaigns each year and embrace what he calls '365-day creativity'. Campbell's vision of virtually continuous creativity was perfectly realized by another advertising agency, Wieden + Kennedy, during the summer of 2010, when it produced a campaign featuring more than 180 short film clips

---

[273] Robert Campbell interview with author, 10 June 2010.

for Procter & Gamble's Old Spice brand. The clips featured Old Spice spokesperson and 'the man you could smell like', former American football star Isaiah Mustafa, sending personal (and often highly amusing) video responses to people who had contacted him via Twitter. His targets included film stars, businesses and media owners. Each of the films was posted on YouTube and new creative executions were created, almost in real time, during an intense few days of filming, to keep the social media community continuously engaged. So when the PR team at Starbucks tweeted Mustafa (who appeared in the films dressed only in a towel), suggesting that he looked cold and needed a coffee, the Wieden + Kennedy team produced a film response within only a few hours, in which Mustafa thanked them for their offer, but said that he preferred to keep himself warm 'by boiling a large pot of water, putting a handful of uncooked lobster tortellini in my mouth and dunking my head in it for 12 to 14 minutes until the tasty seafood delight starts melting in my mouth'.

The Old Spice campaign became a huge viral success story. The total number of web views of all of the campaign videos has now exceeded 110 million, making it the most watched branded video ever to appear on YouTube and, in one of the best tests of viral fame, the campaign has spawned a series of video parodies. According to research company Nielsen, sales of Old Spice during the month of the campaign increased by 107 per cent. Meanwhile, Mustafa became a must-have on the US chat show circuit and has recently landed his first Hollywood movie role. I was particularly struck by the fact that this campaign, featuring multiple creative executions, appeared during the same week that another advertising agency, BBH, resigned the Levi's account that it had held for 28 years. The Levi's brand and the agency's creative reputation had been built on the back of a series of beautifully crafted commercials. It was an event that could be interpreted as marking the end of the advertising epic, to be replaced by the type of faster, cheaper and less polished worked championed by Wieden + Kennedy on Old Spice. The epics will still be produced – Wieden + Kennedy's 'Write the future' ad for Nike during the recent World Cup being a perfect example – but with far less frequency than has previously been the case.

This new reality is not lost on one of the original Mad Men, legendary advertising agency head, Jerry Della Femina. His book *From Those Wonderful Folks Who Gave You Pearl Harbor* – a celebration of the heady, Martini-fuelled days of the ad business in the 1950s and 60s – was the inspiration for the *Mad Men* television series and he is also an adviser to the show's producers. He sounds almost wistful when describing today's more sober, less irresponsible and almost certainly, from his perspective, duller industry: 'Ad budgets are now being cut. The bottom line is now the only line in advertising . . . They [clients] want more and more, and want it to cost less and less. A few 19-year-old students from the School of Visual Arts in New York can design and produce a brilliant campaign in a few hours that once would have taken weeks of late-night creative work by 50 people to produce.'[274]

This faster creative process also forces clients and agencies to air work without extensive pre-testing. This puts much more emphasis on the judgement of the people involved, who can't simply rely on consumer focus groups to help them make their decisions. Campbell provides a note of warning for those who think that this represents an easy alternative: 'If you want

---

[274] Jerry Della Femina, *From Those Wonderful Folks Who Gave You Pearl Harbor: Front-line dispatches from the advertising war*, Canongate Books, 2010.

to think and operate in this way,' he told me, 'you have to have a clear point of view, that everyone on the team understands and a culture that allows people to operate unilaterally, without having to ask their boss permission. Too much advertising is simply bolted-on confection to add interest and lacks integrity. Strategy can't simply be something that is cooked up by an agency planner and tested on a few groups. It has to be true and the client has to be prepared to stand up for it.'

Nike, famously, is a company that never pre-tests its advertising. Scott Bedbury, the company's former worldwide advertising director, says, 'We never pretested anything we did at Nike, none of the ads. [Dan] Wieden [the founder of Wieden + Kennedy] and I had an agreement that as long as our hearts beat, we would never pretest a word of copy. It makes you dull. It makes you predictable. It makes you safe.'[275] Rather than relying on formal market research, Nike encourages its marketers to get out of their offices and test the quality of their ideas with real people. In the words of the company's global brand director Simon Pestridge, 'When anyone in my team comes up with an idea, I tell them to go and run it past a kid on a football pitch. If they don't get laughed at and if they avoid coming across as the kid's un-cool dad, then they're probably on the right track.'[276]

Companies operating outside the software sector have only just begun to get their heads around the benefits and implications of 'living life in beta': a world in which everything is a work in progress. It is a highly disruptive concept: it changes the way we think about the balance of power between owners

---

[275] Quoted in *BusinessWeek*, 7 December 2007.
[276] Quoted in *Revolution* magazine, January 2009.

and consumers of brands and opens up the innovation process to external collaborators. It encourages us to embrace less polished, more authentic and genuine dialogue with customers and challenges our addiction to glossy pieces of marketing perfection. Get it right and, in the spirit of the design industry, you can bring a 'messy vitality' to any institution.

4.4 TIME TO GET REAL

'Decisiveness is about timeliness. And timeliness trumps perfection. The most damaging decisions are missed opportunities, the decisions that didn't get made on time.'

Anne Mulcahy, CEO, Xerox[277]

The CEO of Cisco Systems, John Chambers, has been accused by business journalists of 'loosing his mind'[278] and 'turning the tech giant socialist'.[279] Both comments were intended to be fairly tongue in cheek, but they illustrated the surprise that greeted his decision to restructure his business, devolving decision-making power from a small group of senior executives to a network of cross-functional councils and boards. *Fast Company* magazine described the new structural model as 'a distributed idea engine where leadership emerges organically, unfettered by a central command', and celebrated how Cisco's open and collaborative culture has created 'a laboratory of connectedness and productivity'.[280] Chambers, who was one of John McCain's campaign team – hence *Fast Company*'s cheeky reference to 'socialism' – was driven by a desire to make his company more agile. He believed it needed to move faster (especially in getting products to market), break down internal silos, reinvigorate its innovation processes and help him transform Cisco from 'the plumber of the internet' to more of a consultancy business. In an interview in *McKinsey Quarterly*, he sounded like a man in a hurry, describing how 'all

---

[277] Anne Mulcahy, *McKinsey Quarterly*, 18 May 2010.
[278] Henry Blodget, *Business Insider*, 6 August 2009.
[279] Ellen McGirt, *Fast Company*, 25 November 2008.
[280] Ellen McGirt, *Fast Company*, 25 November 2008.

the windows of opportunities I've missed – areas that got ahead of us that we couldn't get back into without doing big acquisitions or something – have been when I've moved too slow'.[281] One of the more tangible results of his initiative is that business plans that used to take six months to develop and approve, can now be put together in a week. Cisco has started to export its approach to some of its major customers, who will use Cisco technology to help them. Chambers argues that this new devolved decision-making model is actually easier to replicate in other organizations as it is less dependent on the skills of the senior leadership team.

As you might expect from an IT business – especially one responsible for much of the technology at the heart of the global communications network – Chambers and his team have made full use of an array of technologies, from video blogs (preferred by Chambers to the traditional written form, because he is mildly dyslexic) to online discussion forums. He also admits that he has had to change his personal management style in response to very different market conditions: 'I'm a command-and-control guy. It clearly has worked well for me. I say, turn right, 66,600 people turn right. But that's not the future. The future's going to be all around collaboration and teamwork, with a structured process behind it.'[282] This point he makes about the importance of structure is significant. Cisco isn't a freeform, freewheeling operation. It believes in structure, process and discipline, but as an enabler of collaboration and faster decision-making, rather than a constrainer of internal behaviour. The tight system helps Cisco operate in a looser way.

---

[281] John Chambers interview, *McKinsey Quarterly*, August 2010.
[282] John Chambers interview, *McKinsey Quarterly*, August 2010.

Businesses like Cisco are operating in a world in which customers increasingly expect the suppliers of their goods and services to respond almost instantaneously to their demands. This expectation has been driven by the emergence of new technology, especially social media, which facilitates real-time conversations between corporations and their customers. Smart companies are already picking up complaints posted on Twitter (which has become a particularly effective customer complaints channel) and responding almost instantaneously with a commitment to resolve any problems. Train drivers have been known to turn up the air conditioning in rail carriages after their head offices have picked up a critical tweet from an over-heated passenger and relayed a message back to the driver. Within a few years, fuelled by the inevitable growth of smart phones providing instant access to Twitter or similar platforms, this will be the standard practice for the management of all customer complaints, but it is already raising the bar in terms of customer expectations. Taking weeks or even months to deal with a customer complaint through the usual, tortuous internal channels is no longer acceptable.

The all-pervasive influence of new technology is also beginning to change the relationship between politicians and their electorate. The formal Liberal Party leader, David Steel, has described the challenges faced by the modern MP in dealing with the sheer number of emails that are sent to them, compared with the old days of dealing with paper-based correspondence. Not only is it easier to send an email, compared with writing and posting a letter, but people also expect an instant response.[283] Providing the public with instant access to the political decision-makers may be seen by some

---

[283] David Steel interview on BBC Radio 5 Live, 5 August 2010.

commentators as heralding the revitalization of the democratic process, but it also places a huge administrative burden on the political system, both within Westminster and the local constituency offices.

We now find ourselves on the cusp of a business revolution, built around the need to embrace real-time thinking and operating. Andrew Walmsley, co-founder of digital agency i-level, draws an interesting parallel between this and Toyota's introduction of the Just-in-Time production process, which revolutionized the manufacturing sector, reducing waste, improving productivity and allowing a far greater degree of product customization. This innovation, which started as a pragmatic response to the shortage of spare parts in the aftermath of the Second World War, encouraged businesses to be more agile, flexible and responsive to ever-changing market conditions. We are witnessing a similar response to the new challenges posed by the rise of social media. A study by management consultants Booz & Company states, 'The many virtues of digital marketing – its speed, flexibility, interactivity, and accountability – require a whole new set of marketing strategies and skills to make it work . . . It demands a close collaboration between CMOs and CIOs to build technology to automate new marketing processes and provide real-time decision support.'[284] This viewpoint was echoed in a survey of human resources departments, undertaken by *HR* magazine in October 2009, in which it was claimed that, 'HR professionals have seen the future. Organizations will be designed to facilitate lightening-quick decision making. Power will be decentralized. Networked employees will work remotely and

---

[284] Booz & Co. Online Customers, The CMO-CIO Connection, 2009.

flexibly. Creativity will become just as important as productivity and leaders will switch their focus from barking orders to inspiring great ideas.'[285]

Unfortunately, most institutions, whether major corporations or political parties, may have seen the future but cannot even come close to working in real time. This was highlighted in a survey by McKinsey, which revealed that 50 per cent of senior executives claimed that the agility of their organizations was constrained by 'overly centralized, slow, or complex decision-making/approval processes'.[286] Far too many institutions are used to working in their own time, rather than a timeframe dictated by their customers. They are painfully constrained by tortuously long approval processes, legal constraints and organizational practices that leave them incapable of responding in anything other than institutional time, which is measured in days and weeks, rather than minutes. All too often, by the time that all of the evidence necessary to make a decision is assembled and analysed, the original opportunity will probably have disappeared.

Breaking a mindset that you could characterize as 'paralysis by analysis' requires strong leadership. Anne Mulcahy, the former chairman and CEO of Xerox, rescued the business from near bankruptcy. She was also the first woman to be chosen by her peers for the honour of Chief Executive of the Year. When asked by McKinsey to describe how she makes strategic decisions, Mulcahy's answer revealed her appetite for taking risks: 'I would so much rather live with the outcome of making a few bad decisions than miss a boatload of good ones. Some of it flies in the face of good process and just requires

---

[285] 'Head office of the future', *HR* magazine, 1 October 2009.
[286] *McKinsey Quarterly*, June 2006.

good gut.'[287] Her philosophy is shared by General Colin Powell, former chairman of the Joint Chiefs of Staff in George Bush Senior's administration. One of the maxims he has always used throughout his career is the 40–70 rule, whereby he never tries to make a decision without 40 per cent of the information about a particular problem, but doesn't delay any action once he has 70 per cent of the information. His view is that once you get beyond that figure, the time and effort required to increase your knowledge base becomes counter-productive.

Speed in business is becoming recognized as more important than absolute accuracy. BrainJuicer is one of a new generation of research specialists that is responding to the real-time agenda. Its founder John Kearon describes how most businesses, rather than buying research that 'informs, illuminates and inspires better marketing, are simply trying to avoid risk by buying a 120 page insurance policy'.[288] It gives them a comforting illusion of certainty, whereas what they are actually receiving, weeks if not months after the event or opportunity they are trying to measure, is 'heavy on numbers, light on insight and usually dead-on-arrival as far as senior management are concerned'. Kearon is trying to persuade his clients to follow a similar approach to that advocated by Colin Powell, in which it is better to have most of the answer tomorrow than 100 per cent in a few weeks. He talks about his company's mission as 'providing inspiring, illuminating, insightful, impactful, interesting and imaginative research on a quantitative scale, anywhere in the world, with consistent quality and at an affordable price and a hell of a speed'. He is also a strong advocate of the use of psychology and behavioural

---

[287] Anne Mulcahy, *McKinsey Quarterly*, March 2010.
[288] Interview with author, 23 July 2010.

economics to predict human behaviour, rather than the rigid, empirical models that have traditionally been deployed within the research industry.

Predictive Markets is a typical BrainJuicer product, which builds on James Surowiecki's idea of the wisdom of crowds.[289] The company recruits a diverse group of 500 people (their diversity is important) who aren't specifically representative of the target audience – which is contrary to every fundamental principle of good market research – and then plays a game with them in which they imagine that they have shares in a particular idea or product. They then decide, on the basis of the sales pitch that is made to them, whether they would buy further shares or sell what they have already. It has turned out to be a far more effective technique for predicting the likely success of a new product or service, than any of the traditional methods used by research companies. Kearon describes this as challenging the research dogma of 'Me' research – in which you must only ask me about my motivations, behaviour or beliefs – and replacing it with 'We' research. This leverages our skills as social animals, which make us surprisingly good at evaluating and predicting the behaviour of other people. In developing his thinking, Kearon collaborated with Mark Earls, the author of *Herd*, who has become an acknowledged expert on group behaviour. Classic 'Me' research suffers from the 'unreliable narrator' syndrome – the fact that we are pretty rubbish at understanding and articulating our own motivations or understanding our weaknesses. Kearon references a typical research study undertaken in Sweden which found that 50 per cent of Swedish men thought they were among the top 10 per cent of drivers in the country.

---

[289] James Surowiecki, *The Wisdom of Crowds*, Anchor Books, 2005.

This oblique approach to research – not asking the direct opinions of people for whom a product or service is intended – provides a richer, faster and cheaper way of understanding consumer behaviour, opinion and trends. It is particularly effective when comparing the relative merits of good and merely average products. Kearon describes the BrainJuicer approach as 'much looser, less precise, but much better'. This reminded me of another comment, attributed to the research head of a multi-national drinks company, that 'it is better to be broadly right, than precisely wrong', that is to say, they used to measure with huge precision a series of key business metrics which they now realize told them very little about the health of their business. Being only broadly right is highly disturbing for many research and data professionals, but this is the new reality if they want to focus on the things that clearly matter to the fortunes of their businesses.

It would appear that there is a growing appetite for the faster, looser and less precise research championed by the team at BrainJuicer. Kearon describes how 'the penny is starting to drop' with many of his clients. They have witnessed the emergence of real-time technology and its impact on other areas of their business and seen the incredible speed at which information can travel through social media. When news of a major incident can be transmitted around the globe within minutes, it feels incredibly anachronistic to have to wait weeks for a report detailing the success, or otherwise, of your latest product. Businesses are also, in the words of Nestle's head of market research, Denyse Drummond-Dunn, 'drowning in research, yet thirsty for knowledge'.[290] In my experience, there seems to be a simple truth in business that the companies that

---

[290] Quoted by John Kearon in his Esomar 2009 paper, 'Me-to-we Research'.

spend the most money on research and analysis have the fewest insights. In contrast, I love the response of Willie Davidson, the grandson of the founder of the Harley Davidson Company, when he was once asked by a reporter, 'Do you do any market research to learn more about the wants and needs of your customers?' He replied: 'Oh sure, we stay in constant contact with our customers. We ride with them all the time.'[291]

Kearon is also an advocate of using the real-time research feedback provided by Google Trends, what he describes as 'research without repondents'. Whether tracking the spread of swine flu across the globe or the hype surrounding Susan Boyle's appearance on *Britain's Got Talent*, this readily accessible source of real-time data has the potential to transform the research industry. In the case of swine flu, certain search terms typed by Google users have proven to be highly accurate indicators of latent flu activity. Google has now created Google Flu Trends, using aggregated search data, to estimate current flu activity around the world, in near-real time. This is far faster than the surveillance data published by the official providers of health information and probably more accurate. It can also be accessed by anyone with an internet connection, not simply the medical experts.

Twitter is also proving to be a highly effective alternative to traditional types of research. The vast majority of tweets may be completely inane, but, taken as a whole and with the right monitoring tools, Twitter is a brilliantly useful, real-time barometer of popular opinion. During the post-election unrest in Iran in 2009 and in the absence of any official US government

---

[291] Referenced in Mack Collier's blog http://www.mpdailyfix.com/blurring-the-lines/

presence in Iran, Twitter, YouTube, Facebook and other social media sites were used to access the sort of information normally provided by embassy staff. It may not have been as reliable as having people on the ground, but it was certainly a lot safer. In television, the emerging habit of tweeting along with your favourite programme has given broadcasters an immediate gauge of whether their programmes are engaging the audience. This won't challenge the primacy of the official audience ratings systems – at least in the short term – but when a show starts becoming a trending topic on Twitter, broadcasters have a pretty good idea that they have a hit on their hands. Similarly, it used to take the Hollywood film studios two or three days after a premiere before they knew whether they had a hit or a miss on their hands. Now, by tracking comments on social media, they know within hours.

The Football Association has suffered more than most institutions in recent years from negative publicity. The politics of football are tricky at the best of times, but a revolving door of chairmen and chief executives, accompanied by the type of juicy sex scandals that keep the tabloids happy, has made the FA want to be seen to be in control of events, rather than at their mercy. So when the time came to announce the England squad that would be going to the World Cup in South Africa in 2010, it was decided that tight news management would be the order of the day. The players not selected would be spoken to in advance, the important people in blazers would hear the news before it became public knowledge and the press announcements would be cleared by an army of PR professionals and lawyers. Unfortunately, the FA failed to allow for the Twitter effect. News of the non-selection of Theo Walcott had already appeared on the microblogging platform before the announcement had been made public.

In fact, the names of all of the players excluded from the final tournament squad were being widely shared over the internet before the FA's PR machine finally cranked into action. In the old days you could issue a story under an embargo and be reasonably confident that it would be respected by the traditional media. Now in a real-time world, when everyone is a potential journalist – including footballers, their agents and random hangers-on – stories can emerge and spread in seconds. The FA discovered, like so many traditional institutions, that you no longer have the luxury of working to a timescale defined by your internal processes and procedures.

The core characteristics of successful institutions are now speed, responsiveness and agility, which means that the ability to improvise is more useful than the ability to deliberate. This represents a huge challenge for most institutions, which have allowed themselves, over many decades, to become bound up in layers of often pointless bureaucracy, tortuous decision-making processes and legal safeguards. It is no wonder that most struggle to cope with a social media-empowered world of instant access and instant response. In the words of Rupert Murdoch, 'The world is changing very fast. Big will not beat small anymore. It will be the fast beating the slow.'[292]

---

[292] Quoted in *Fast Company*, 4 February 2008.

4.5 THE COLLABORATIVE CORPORATION

*'One of the interesting things here is that the people who should
be shaping the future are politicians. But the political framework itself is so dead and closed that people look to other
sources, like artists, because art and music allow people a
certain freedom.'*

Thom Yorke, Radiohead[293]

The Threadless T-shirt company is a business built on the
virtues of collaboration. It has also become one of the most
avidly studied case studies in America's business schools,
which is pretty remarkable given the fact that it is a relatively
small online retailer, selling something as mundane as
T-shirts. There are thousands of businesses selling similar
products, but what makes Threadless so interesting is its
community-based business model, which many experts
believe will become the template for the next generation of
online entrepreneurs.

The company started as a hobby for two Chicago-based
designers, Jake Nickell and Jacob DeHart. Nickell had won a
T-shirt design competition staged by the New Media Underground festival, an informal gathering of web designers in
London in 2000. He and DeHart were sufficiently inspired to
start running similar competitions in their spare time. They
both put in $500 to set up the business and print the first batch
of T-shirts, selected from designs submitted by the 100 people
who entered their first competition. Within a few years they
had taken the plunge, dropped out of college (in the case of
Nickell) and started building an online business, which today

---

[293] Thom Yorke interviewed in *Resonance* magazine, Issue 39, 2003.

boasts over one million members and sales in excess of
$30 million. This isn't simply providing an opportunity for
people outside the company to submit the occasional suggestion
which might be implemented, or enter a one-off design competition. It is a new type of community business, which
requires no professional designers, no sales force, no distribution, no market research and no advertising. This also means
that even though the T-shirts only cost around $18 the profit
margins are extremely healthy. Hundreds of designs are submitted each week, the community votes, the favourite designs
are put into production and the successful designers are
rewarded with $2,000 in cash, a $500 voucher and a further
$500 in cash each time their design is reprinted. The company
has to date printed 800 different T-shirt designs, chosen from
ideas submitted by 80,000 professional and amateur artists.
The business is owned as much by the community as by
Nickell, DeHart and their investors. In fact, the vast majority
of the company's employees started out as community
members. Designers are encouraged to do their own marketing
and provided with templates to produce their own advertising.
The company doesn't even require that designers hand over
the copyright on their submitted work.

Most of the Threadless community is highly active, not
simply buying T-shirts but also participating in the weekly
votes. There is a forum for prospective designers to test rough
or beta versions of their designs with members of the Threadless community before they are submitted. The community
has also spawned a large number of off-shoots, including the
Loves Threadless blog; Rethreaded, a website for fans to
discuss previous designs and sell shirts they no longer want;
and even more bizarrely, Threadless Cakes, in which people
post photos of cakes inspired by some of the T-shirt designs.

It is this vibrant and self-sustaining community that has started to excite the business experts. Harvard Business School professor Karim Lakhani says, 'We thought that open source could only work in software and now it is being applied to a product as mundane as a T-shirt.'[294]

The success of Threadless has encouraged many imitators of its collaborative design model, including Minted.com, which runs design contests for its high-end stationery business. As with Threadless, designers are invited to submit their work and the best designs are selected by the Minted community. Jeff Howe, the author of *Crowdsourcing*,[295] believes that these techniques work particularly well for design-based business because of the relatively low barriers to entry: 'You have a lot of people who can do low-end design. You know they can create a logo. They can lay out a web page, even though they're not professionals. They're adequate enough that they can make a supplementary income doing it or do it for fun.'[296] There is also a vibrant freelance design community more than happy to supplement their income with this type of initiative. It is interesting to debate where this leaves the traditional design agency. Why use expensive design agencies, when work can be sourced from the open market at a fraction of the price? Design agency heads can try to argue that their creative product is superior – better researched, more carefully crafted – but they may be fighting a losing battle.

During the summer of 2009, Unilever – which tends to set the marketing trends that other brand owners follow – decided

---

[294] *Inc.* magazine, 1 June 2008.
[295] Jeff Howe, *Crowdsourcing: Why the power of the crowd is driving the future of business*, Random House Business, 2009.
[296] Quoted in CNET News, 29 August 2008.

to abandon the usual practice of deploying an advertising agency on one of its leading brands, Peperami. It dismissed the agency that had worked on the brand for 15 years and created the successful 'bit of an animal' campaign and instead offered a prize of $10,000 to any creative team that could come up with the best-executed idea. Some in the industry dismissed this as a cynical attempt to get creative work on the cheap, but the Unilever team was insistent that this looser approach was a genuine attempt to bring some innovation to the sourcing of ideas. Although the Unilever spokesperson claimed that the winning idea could come from a 'plumber from Barnsley', the fact that the contest was being run through an online community for creatives called ideabounty.com suggested that Unilever wanted to attract entries from professional creative teams. The company also promoted the competition on the freelance recruitment sections of the major advertising and marketing blogs. It was therefore hardly surprising that the winning entry didn't come from a Barnsley plumber, but from a former agency creative director working alongside a freelance copywriter.

The Peperami experiment proved so successful that Unilever has decided to apply the approach to 13 of its most important global brands. For a mere £7,000 (which is the prize for the suppliers of the winning ideas), Unilever will be able to acquire hours of creative content. And even if most of it is complete rubbish, there is bound to be some decent material, and all for the cost of a typical day's photo-shoot or a creative director's bar bill at Cannes. Agencies can protest that this undervalues the strategic thinking and creative originality that their expensively assembled teams can bring to a brief, but it is likely to fall on deaf ears. Creative agencies are already over-reliant on freelance talent and clients have realized that they can access great creative thinking, without paying expensive agency overheads. This makes even more sense when, as is the case with Peperami, there is an existing creative idea that simply demands new executions. Why pay for planners and account handlers when most of the strategic thinking has already been done? Nic Ray, speaking on behalf of the freelance creative community, underlines why Unilever's initiative is so smart: 'I feel compelled to point out that almost all agency creatives work on freelance briefs outside of their normal employ – and get paid substantially less than $10k for doing so. Here's an opportunity to work on one of the UK's most iconic (and irreverent) brands, pull out those brilliant back draw ideas that were never sold and have some fun shaking up the industry in the process.'[297]

O2 AND MUTUAL GIVING

The community-based approach is also being used by the UK's largest mobile network operator, O2, which has created an innovative subsidiary in the form of giffgaff. The company, named after the Scottish term for 'mutual giving', was launched in November 2009. It describes itself as being built on a 'people-powered' model in which customers are not only involved in everything the company does, but can also share in its financial success. The company's wonderfully homespun manifesto says, 'We believe in listening to our members. Involving them. Being run by them. Rewarding them with money. The idea is that if we all work together, we can really go places, not least to that Utopian place called

---

[297] Blog posting on *Brand Republic*, 26 August 2009.

Cheapersimplerfairercommunicating. (Hey, don't stamp on our dream: there is such a place.)'[298]

Members of the giffgaff community are rewarded with points for recruiting new members, contributing ideas, responding to requests for feedback or helping other people resolve problems with their mobile phones. They were even provided with a set of online tools to create their own video clips to support the giffgaff launch. Every six months the points accumulated by members are converted into cash prizes, which they can take themselves or donate to charity. To date, around 20 per cent of people signing up for giffgaff have been actively involved in the community. The company's stated ambition is that one in five community members will get half of the cost of their calls back by getting involved. They won't earn enough to give up their day jobs – the company announced recently that one of its members had earned £750 from helping out other giffgaff members over the past few months – but it is a tangible demonstration of the value of co-ownership. The company plans to involve community members in an increasing number of key business decisions, from pricing models to marketing campaigns.

Gav Thompson, O2's head of brand strategy, and the originator of the giffgaff concept, claims that he came up with the idea during a web 2.0 conference in San Francisco: 'At the conference, I had been impressed by the case study of President Obama's campaign [that was still running at the time] managing to successfully activate communities via the web. Twitter was also on the agenda, but a few hours in, I was zoning out while hearing about endless big brands that were rather clumsily jumping on the bandwagon. The idea for

[298] www.giffgaff.com/manifesto

giffgaff did literally fly into my head, and I wrote down "mutual, simple and fair" as the three founding principles.'[299] Thompson is clearly a highly persuasive individual: his radical new business model, albeit underpinned by extensive consumer research, was given immediate approval by his board. He is in no doubt that backing giffgaff allows O2 to tap into an important consumer trend: 'There is an ongoing rise in free thinkers – consumers who demand more interaction and engagement with the brands they use, preferring smaller businesses to large corporations . . . people want to be more involved with brands . . . and online people recommendation is now more highly valued than brand advertising . . . Where eBay, Wikipedia and Facebook have led the way, giffgaff is now trailblazing for mobile. It's the mobile service for people who want to feel more involved in the brands they use.'[300] This is how one community member described his motivation for signing up to giffgaff: 'Good product, good pricing, but by far the most exiting part for me is the opportunity to earn hard cash for promoting what is essentially the best thing since sliced bread.'[301]

Giffgaff's operating model, which is not reliant on call centres or expensive marketing campaigns and product support functions allows it to be much more nimble and agile than its competitors. It also provides O2 and its parent company Telefonica with a challenger sub-brand, capable of appealing to the types of people demanding a different kind of relationship with the companies that supply their goods and services or those simply alienated by the big, corporate suppliers. As

---

[299] Quoted in www.thereallymobileproject.com, 29 June 2010.
[300] Gav Thompson interview in *Contagious* magazine, February 2010.
[301] www.giffgaff.com

you might expect, giffgaff abides by the principles of transparency. It has a live Twitter feed on its home page featuring comments about the company, both positive and negative. Potential customers are also invited to check out the views of existing members on its online forums.

The rock group Radiohead has also taken the idea of community collaboration to create a new type of business model and helped to create a completely new way to commercialize music. When the band launched their seventh album – the critically acclaimed *In Rainbows* – they invited fans to download an initial MP3 version at whatever price they thought appropriate. Rather than abuse this offer, Radiohead's fans appear to have been driven by a spirit of fairness, paying, on average, around £4 to download the album. More than one million fans took up the offer, pocketing Radiohead over £4 million in less than a week. And because the band was no longer under contract to a major record label, it did not have to give away a significant percentage of the profits. The album was subsequently released in traditional CD and vinyl formats and the band also issued a premium priced, deluxe version of the album featuring vinyl LPs, extra songs, photos and a hardback book of artwork and lyrics. This initiative even made the pages of *BusinessWeek*, with columnist Rick Wartzman suggesting that even Peter Drucker, one of the original management gurus, would have approved of this radical pricing model.[302]

The band also broke with the convention of hiring top directors to film their promo videos, by inviting members of the public to produce an animated video for any track on the album. People with great ideas but without the technical skills

---

[302] Rick Wartzman, *BusinessWeek*, 11 October 2007.

necessary to create a video were encouraged to collaborate with more technically proficient fans on the animation-sharing site Aniboom. Radiohead's co-managers Bryce Edge and Chris Hufford were named innovators of the year in the 2008 MediaGuardian Awards for Innovation, with the judges praising them for the way that they had 'managed to revolutionise the way music is sold and marketed almost overnight'.[303] It was also seen as symbolizing a shift of power within the music industry, as Chris Parry, founder of Fiction records, recalled, 'The music companies used to have a monopoly when it came to finding new talent and distributing songs. Now artists such as Radiohead are beginning to challenge the status quo. New technology has subverted the way the majors used to do business. The balance of power has shifted from the companies to the fans and artists.'[304] The smart businesses are the ones like Radiohead, Threadless and giffgaff that have recognized and embraced this power shift and tapped into the collective instinct.

---

[303] *Guardian*, 7 March 2008.
[304] Quoted in the *Guardian*, 7 October 2007.

4.6 RETHINKING BRANDING

'Branding is a disastrous metaphor. Anything indelibly branded can become a real liability.'
> John Grant, *The New Marketing Manifesto*[305]

Lego is one of the world's great brands. Creativity is one of its core values and it has encouraged millions of fans around the world to come up with their own uses for the bricks, design new products or produce their own animated videos featuring the iconic mini-figures. The pitch it makes to creative thinkers is wonderfully compelling: 'Welcome inventors, explorers, tinkerers, artists and idea people of all ages! This is a little place on the internet devoted to the moment when the brain suddenly finds the answer you've been seeking. The moment all the pieces come together. We call it CLICK. And it's what we do here in this factory of ours.'[306] It is a message that has resonated with a wide range of creative and technological communities, as well as complete amateurs. Unfortunately, you cannot set limits or constraints on people's creativity, so when spoof Lego advertisements started appearing online featuring a heroin addict shooting up with the caption, 'Kids shouldn't watch too much TV' or an image of the Twin Towers collapsing with the headline, 'Rebuild it', both accompanied by a prominent Lego logo, there wasn't much that the company could do about it.

Less controversially, but equally challenging for Lego, has been the behaviour of many of its most avid fans. Something

---

[305] John Grant, *The New Marketing Manifesto: The 12 rules for building successful brands in the 21st century*, Texere Publishing, 2009.
[306] www.lego.com

as simple as changing the colour of some of its bricks, in an attempt to improve their appeal to children, created a huge backlash from many collectors, who complained that the new colours were no longer compatible with the old. An attempt to involve another group of fans in a new product development programme also backfired when the company attempted to get them to sign a non-disclosure agreement, which, according to brand consultant and author Martin Kornberger 'introduced a sense of hierarchy and exclusion, at odds with the free sharing that is a hallmark of open-source communities'.[307] As far as he is concerned, it is 'next to impossible' for Lego to control or institutionalize its fan groups, but instead it needs to find a way to share control.

A huge industry has emerged, especially during the past twenty years, dedicated to developing, nurturing and measuring the fortunes of brands. You can understand why when you realize how much of the value of the world's leading corporations is locked up in these intangible brand assets: *Fortune* magazine put the figure at 72 per cent and in some categories the percentage of corporate value accounted for by its brands tops 85 per cent. Young & Rubicam's John Gerzema and Edward Lebar have suggested that the growth in the intangible value assigned to the world's leading brands by the financial markets risks creating a $4 trillion 'brand bubble' with the increasingly inflated valuations losing all connection with their true commercial value: 'On the one hand Wall Street, investors and brand executives believe that brands have limitless potential that will continue to drive already burgeoning enterprise and market values. On the other, consumers are

---

[307] Martin Kornberger, 'How brand communities influence innovation and culture', *Market Leader*, Q3 2010.

sending out signals that they are no longer enamoured of many of our brands and are not committed to future loyalty.'[308]

The branding industry – populated by consultants, strategists, designers and far too many gurus – is underpinned by the illusion of control and inviolability. It is built on the naïve belief that a brand's image and positioning can be set in stone and protected from any outside interference, while its consumers will treat it with reverence and respect. How else can you explain the painfully slow and costly way in which most brands are developed and managed and the huge amount of pseudo-science used to justify what are invariably subjective or intuitive decisions? Marketing teams, supported by branding consultants and design experts, spend months agonizing over a brand's positioning, deploying a vast array of methodologies and processes, with strange names such as 'brand onions' and 'brand keys'. They then spend hours in workshops, brainstorms and focus groups in an attempt to define a brand's core values, essence and customer proposition. The meaning and nuance of particular words is debated at ridiculous length. Once some form of consensus has been reached on the brand's features, values and proposition, typefaces and visuals are crafted with the diligence of a medieval monk working on an early edition of the Bible. Enormous documents are produced to specify the exact rules that must be followed when using the company logo on every conceivable application. Brand policemen within the marketing department are selected to prevent internal abuses of the sacred brand identity while intellectual property departments are tasked with cracking down on trademark violations from people or organizations outside the business.

---

[308] John Gerzema and Edward Lebar, *The Brand Bubble: The looming crisis in brand value and how to avoid it*, Jossey Bass, 2008.

Brand managers huddle over 'dashboards' featuring a range of brand tracking metrics, like Bond villains plotting global domination, deluding themselves that they can somehow control the fortunes of their precious brands by making subtle adjustments to their marketing plans. Meanwhile, back in the real world, consumers are busy subverting this introspective, time-consuming and, quite frankly, delusional branding process.

As described earlier in this book, institutions increasingly have to accommodate the subversive and creative impulses of today's consumers. If you want a simple illustration of this, try typing some of the word's most famous brand names into Google Images and see what you get – although, be warned, some of the images that appear towards the top of the rankings are not very pleasant. One of the first images you see when you type in Microsoft is of someone urinating on a Microsoft company sign. And if you are so inclined, one of the first images you see when you type in the name of one of the world's leading payment card brands is pornographic. There are plenty of search marketing specialists out there with advice on how to manipulate the Google Images search algorithm, to ensure that the more flattering images appear towards the top of the search rankings. Google also offers an image removal service, although this requires the participation of the owners of the website hosting the offending image, which is clearly not an option in many of the more extreme cases of creative self-expression. The final resort for companies or brands who believe that their reputation is being seriously damaged by negative images is to involve the corporate lawyers, but in a world in which the principles of self-expression and free speech are vigorously defended, this is invariably counter-productive.

The Google Images test and the challenge Lego faces in dealing with one particular form of creative expression, are perfect illustrations of how, in the real world – as opposed to the artificial world of brand planning – brands cannot be kept in splendid isolation, immune from the creative whims of their critics, or more often their most enthusiastic supporters. Even the IPA, the voice of the British advertising industry, recommended in a recent report that 'brands must appear more humble'. The people responsible for developing and nurturing the world's leading brands have to come to terms with an era in which people's apparently insatiable desire to personalize and manipulate all forms of creative content coincides with a virtually unlimited technological capability that allows even the most ham-fisted amateur, given the right amount of commitment, to produce high-quality work. American motivational writer Earl Nightingale said that, 'Creativity is a natural extension of our enthusiasm.' This enthusiasm can be encouraged, harnessed but never controlled. Creativity has been democratized, although as demonstrated by the Google Images test, the effects are not always benign.

Consumer empowerment evangelists have long argued that brand managers may own trademarks, but that the true ownership of a brand resides with those consumers who talk about it, blog about it, attend its events, join social networks devoted to it, share and customize its creative messages and, in the case of some iconic brands such as Harley Davidson, tattoo its logos on their bodies. Alex Wipperfurth, the author of *Brand Hijack*,[309] goes so far as to suggest that brand owners should let the market hijack their brands by allowing customers to shape

---

[309] Alex Wipperfurth, *Brand Hijack: Marketing without marketing*, Portfolio, 2005.

the brands' meaning: 'Let go of the fallacy that the brand belongs to you. It belongs to the market,' although his message is one of flexibility rather than abdication: 'carefully plan every step but be totally open to having the story rewritten along the way.' There is an emerging consensus that brand building should be seen as a collaborative process, shared with a brand's end-users and other stakeholders. But does this mean that institutions should hand over control of their brands entirely to outside influences? Mike Beverland, professor of marketing at Bath University, argues that while marketers can't dictate, or control brand meaning in a world where consumers will use brands as they feel fit and create their own narratives around them, neither should they accept total consumer supremacy.[310] He has come up with the term 'negotiated brand meaning' to explain the balancing act, in which brand managers need to see themselves as directing the 'brand process' rather than determining a 'brand positioning'. In his view, the idea of a brand taking a 'position' is too inflexible in a fast-changing world.

Handing over your brand to its consumers may sound like a fine idea in principle, but allowing them to define entirely what the brand stands for betrays a fundamental weakness on the part of the brand owner. Marketing professor Mark Ritson says that if 'you don't stand for anything, you get eaten alive by competitors who do . . . We are attracted to substance – not vague and open assertions of empowerment and affection. You must represent something specific to a particular segment or you will lose'.[311] *Times* business journalist Sathnam Sanghera described this phenomenon of taking consumer-generated

---

[310] Mike Beverland, *Building Brand Authenticity*, Palgrave Macmillan, 2009.
[311] *Marketing* magazine, 13 October 2009.

content to its logical conclusion as risking the 'blandness of interactivity'.[312] I am all for a participative approach to brand development and planning – a brand's most passionate supporters should have a stake in the articulation of what the brand stands for – but I share Sanghera's criticism of brand owners who 'have simultaneously decided that it is not up to them to decide what their brand offers consumers but it is up to consumers to decide what they want the brand to be'.[313]

Successful brands have a clearly articulated point of view and values that shape everything that they do. They do not constantly define themselves according to the prevailing mood of their consumers. While a brand's most passionate supporters should have a stake in the articulation of what the brand stands for, simply treating it as a blank canvas upon which its consumers can express themselves smacks of abdication, rather than collaboration. In a sense, the dangers facing brand owners seeking to embrace consumer empowerment are similar to those of a politician who is tempted to always give the electorate what it wants. This is fine in the short term, but such a populist approach rarely earns the respect of voters in the longer term. In fact, the term 'populist politician' is invariably used as shorthand for someone regarded as weak and unprincipled. The same is true of 'populist brands'; they may aspire to universal affection, but they are fundamentally weak.

Brands are dynamic and malleable. It is illogical that they should be governed by tight rules and regulations or over-prescriptive, linear planning methodologies. Christian Barnett, planning director of design agency Coley Porter Bell, asserts

---

[312] Sathnam Sanghera, *The Times*, 28 September 2009.
[313] Sathnam Sanghera, *The Times*, 28 September 2009.

that, 'The spirit or essence of a brand is more important than the brand guidelines. It is this which ensures a creative coherence for everything that the brand does, not some arbitrary set of rules.'[314] This is a critically important point. If companies spent a fraction of the time that they allocate to producing and policing brand guidelines on defining, building and nurturing a culture that supports their brand values, they would be far more successful. But as already discussed, building a strong internal culture takes time and effort, whereas issuing rules, even though they are likely to be completely ignored once they leave the sanctuary of the head office, seems much simpler.

One business that has adopted a looser branding model is Google. The company breaks just about every principle of protecting an intellectual property by changing the design of its logo on an almost daily basis. The company describes these 'decorative changes' to the Google logo as 'doodles' and talks about how: 'Having a little bit of fun with the corporate logo by redesigning it from time to time is unheard of at many companies but at Google, it is a part of the brand.'[315] The doodles began in 1999 when the company's founders wanted to create a version of their logo to mark their attendance at the Burning Man festival in Nevada and send a message to colleagues that they were out of the office. Since this time, over 1,000 versions have been created and the company actively encourages creative doodle suggestions from fans. Not only does this generate interest in the business – there are even blogs dedicated to showcasing the Google design – but it is almost an invitation to play with Google's intellectual property.

---

[314] Christian Barnett interview with author, 18 June 2010.
[315] www.google.com

Google's intellectual property experts are either very smart or very lazy (I would like to think the former), because they are adopting a far looser approach to the protection of their trademark than is the norm. The idea that brands are flexible or malleable entities which consumers should be encouraged to manipulate or customize gives most intellectual property lawyers sleepless nights. The current legal convention is that the owner of an intellectual property, such as a corporate logo, needs to be seen to be doing everything in their power to protect that property from abuse, otherwise their ownership can be challenged. This is why legal departments have always been quick to stamp on any abuses, whether it is a local restaurant business using the 'Mc' prefix, which McDonald's believes that it owns, or the manufacturers of T-shirts featuring customized versions of the Nike swoosh or similar marks. In 1962, Coca-Cola's lawyers slapped a cease and desist order on Andy Warhol for producing one of his iconic screenprint images featuring Coca-Cola bottles. Not even Warhol was allowed to put his personal stamp on the Coca-Cola brand. It would be nice to think that things have moved on since the 1960s, but the defenders of intellectual property continue to create problems for their marketing colleagues, especially when it comes to trying to protect the integrity of brands from the creative enthusiasm of the people who consume them. The legal experts have yet to work out how to manage intellectual properties in today's hyper-connected, rights-abusing world: a world in which spoof advertising campaigns are created to subvert or mock brands; in which a political party can be elected to the European Parliament on a platform of file-sharing rights and the relaxation of copyright laws; and in which any attempt to resort to legal action, in defence of intellectual property, is regarded as an attack on free speech.

In an all too typical case, a group of people at UK digital agency Poke were issued with a cease and desist order by Mars for having the temerity to create an unauthorized fan site for the company's Snickers chocolate brand. This was a purely non-commercial venture, intended to showcase the agency's skills and provide some fun for its creative team. The site allowed people to produce customized versions of the Snickers logo. Not only did it attract 80,000 visitors – who we have to assume were Snickers fans – but it also provided a link to the official Snickers site. Most marketers would be delighted with this level of consumer interaction with their brand, but the lawyers decided the need to protect the brand's intellectual property was too important to allow them to give free creative rein to fans.

The activist community has been quick to spot how easy it is to goad the legal advisers working for the multinational corporations into action by appearing to threaten the integrity of their brands. Brand or company logos in particular are highly precious things and these core elements of a brand's intangible value can be worth hundreds of millions of pounds. It is therefore hardly surprising that the intellectual property experts invariably over-react when they believe the brand's integrity to be under threat. Greenpeace has proved itself to be particularly adept at courting and then exploiting this tendency. It has been involved in a long-running battle with Nestle about the way that the company sources palm oil for its chocolate brands. To highlight what it considered to be an unethical sourcing policy that was destroying the rainforest habit of the orang-utans, Greenpeace produced a spoof version of Nestle's Kit-Kat logo, swapping the brand name for the word 'Killer' in the same typeface as Kit-Kat. It then produced a video featuring an office worker eating a Kit-Kat, only to discover that he was chewing on the bloody finger of an orang-utan, rather than a piece of chocolate. These types of campaign, with no advertising media investment to support them, require the oxygen of publicity to make them effective. As if on cue, the Nestle legal advisers stepped up to supply the oxygen. They demanded any comments on Facebook featuring the spoof 'Killer' logo were removed on the grounds of breaching intellectual property and forced YouTube to stop featuring the Greenpeace video. Predictably, this action simply trans-formed a relatively low-key activist protest into a global media story. The problem was exacerbated by the actions of one of the Nestle communications team who decided to engage in a debate on Facebook with the company's critics. Unfortunately, what started as an exchange of views became increasingly heated.

The marketers and corporate communications people at Nestle aren't stupid – they are simply facing new communi-cations challenges for which the standard legal conventions and practices are no longer appropriate. Freedom of expression may be a problem for lawyers but it is taken seriously in the social media space. Blocking or deleting online content you don't like is invariably counter-productive, no matter what the lawyers say. People will still find the content. As the spokes-woman from Greenpeace said of Nestle's actions: 'They've made it so easy for us.'[316]

When Greenpeace, fresh from its battles with Nestle, decided to join the attack on BP at the height of the Gulf of Mexico disaster, its chosen target was the BP brand. It created a perfect 'red rag' for the BP 'bull' by encouraging consumers

---

[316] Tracy Frauzel, head of digital communications at Greenpeace, quoted in *Communicate* magazine, 19 March 2010.

to create their own versions of the Beyond Petroleum logo. Dick Close, a US-based artist who submitted an image of an oil-coated duck, pointed out that, 'Graphic design has always been a part of social protest.'[317] A dedicated microsite was created as a platform for professional and amateur designers to express their anger and create their own versions of the helios logo. This tactic had particular resonance because the 'Beyond Petroleum' tagline – the idea that this is a business committed to non-traditional energy sources – looked even less credible in the wake of an environmental disaster. Greenpeace was clearly hoping that BP's lawyers would follow the lead taken by their counterparts at Nestle, and attack the initiative on the grounds of trademark infringement. For once, the lawyers were smart enough not to take the bait.

The legal profession, particularly that part of it responsible for protecting trademarks and other aspects of intellectual property, needs a collective response to the new era of subversive consumer behaviour, democratized creativity, the lack of respect for traditional sources of authority and of course the all-pervasive influence of the internet. But they need to be joined by the whole branding industry in a collective rethink about the way that they develop and nurture brands. There is nothing wrong with brand-planning methodologies, just so long as they are seen as what they are – tools to help structure thinking and guide future activity. There is also nothing wrong with taking a strategic approach to the articulation of a brand's positioning, so long as it doesn't soak up hours of management time in needless discussions. These are exciting times for the branding industry – consumers want to collaborate, social media is opening up new platforms for engagement and,

---

[317] Quoted in the *Observer*, 11 July 2010.

notwithstanding the risk of a brand bubble, brand valuations continue to rise. It just needs to stop being so slow, ponderous, introspective and arrogant and take note of the words of Mark Ritson: 'The biggest brand of them all, Coke, was built not from market analysis but by a potty pharmacist brewing medicinal tonic in his back yard using nothing more than instinct and a three-legged brass kettle.'[318]

---

[318] Mark Ritson, *Marketing* magazine, 20 May 2009.

CHAPTER 5

MAKING LOOSE WORK

'A lot of people write their stuff down and then develop it, but I'm inordinately lazy. I have great difficulty writing things down. In the end, I develop bits of material and then, in between those bits, I take the courage to break off, a bit like a jazz musician saying, "I'm going to go off on a solo here, I haven't got a band, it's just me."'

Eddie Izzard in an interview by Bono
in the *Independent*, 16 May 2006

This book was never intended as a libertarian's charter. A successful business, or any other venture for that matter, cannot be entirely loose. There has to be some structure or an organizing principle: a framework in which loose thinking and working can thrive. The type of structure that is required will vary, depending on the nature of the organization and the space it which it operates. A pharmaceutical company, operating in a highly regulated environment, in which mistakes can be literally life-threatening and senior managers put in prison if they break the rules, can never be as loose as a business selling low-risk consumer products or a grassroots community group. But equally, it cannot be entirely tight if it is to thrive in the modern world, retain the best people, harness their creativity and deal with its critics. Regulatory constraints demand caution but not inaction. Some degree of looseness can be built into any organization. It is simply a question of finding the right tight–loose balance.

We witnessed a perfect illustration of this during the Ryder Cup in 2008. One of the biggest decisions facing the two Ryder Cup captains is the order in which they send out their players on the final day. Do you start with your stronger performers or hold them back until later in the day? Following a terrible final-day performance by the European team, when they were soundly beaten by their American rivals, it was revealed that the captain, Nick Faldo, allowed his players to decide where they wanted to appear; they dictated his strategy and Faldo appeared to abdicate his role as key decision-maker. Some might regard this as a smart example of employee empowerment, notwithstanding Europe's defeat, but compare Faldo's approach with that of his rival captain, Paul Azinger. The US captain certainly consulted his players but admitted that his team's final-day line-up had 'been in his head for two weeks'. He listened to his team of highly paid, often egotistical golfers, but the final decision was down to him.

Another sporting parallel helps to make the point about the need to find a balance between tight and loose. Rugby Union is a relatively complex sport and, to the uninformed, the activity on the pitch can look bewilderingly chaotic. Rugby coaches rely on repetitive drills to help players work together more effectively as a unit. In a similar way to the drilling of troops for battle, endless hours are spent on the training ground practising set plays. The aim is that every player knows what is expected of him in a particular situation and can act, almost without thinking. A rugby lineout, for example, requires the thrower of the ball, the catcher and the people lifting him to be in perfect harmony, which can only happen after hours of practice – and in the case of the Welsh team that I follow, not even then.

Without an organizing framework at the heart of every rugby team, it would simply degenerate into chaos. But the truly successful teams need something more than this framework, otherwise they risk becoming too predictable. Set plays, rehearsed in the artificial environment of the training ground, often without any opposition, all too often break down in the real match situation. The more enlightened coaches therefore talk about the need for 'heads up rugby' or 'playing the game in front of you'. What they mean is that players have to be able to make decisions in the heat of the action on the pitch, rather than always follow pre-programmed moves. This is a perfect example of freedom within a framework. But it takes a great deal of hard work and inspiration to get players to actually deliver 'heads up rugby'. They have to be given the skills and confidence to judge situations, make decisions and take calculated risks. The legendary Scottish coach Jim Greenwood, who virtually invented modern rugby coaching, described it as 'well-judged risk-taking',[319] which is probably as good a definition of the art of management as you will find in any business book.

We also need to heed James Boyle's warning about the risk of 'cultural agoraphobia' which 'leads us always to emphasise the downsides of openness and lack of central control and to overvalue the virtues of order and authority'.[320] The old IT

---

[319] Jim Greenwood, *Total Rugby: Fifteen-man rugby for coach and player*, A&C Black, 2003.
[320] James Boyle, *The Public Domain: Enclosing the commons of the mind*, Yale University Press, 2009.

cliché was 'no one ever gets sacked by buying IBM' and by the same token, managers tend not to be criticized for advocating stronger compliance, auditing and approval procedures; similarly, politicians are usually praised in the media when they advocate the imposition of yet more legislation. Fighting the natural human instinct to tighten up, especially when the going gets tough, requires strong leadership and probably more bravery than is typically found in the executive suite. But having spent the past couple of years exploring this topic, I am convinced that there are more than enough powerful examples of institutions that have thrived by embracing looser ways of thinking and working. They believe in the virtues of pragmatism, collaboration, dialogue and transparency and that long-established business rules are made to be broken.

This iconoclastic spirit is perfectly encapsulated by engineer and entrepreneur James Dyson's approach to new product development: 'When we start a project we deliberately do the wrong thing. If you do the right thing, the logical thing, all you are doing is following the same path as everyone else.'[321] These loose organizations have come to terms with the chaos and ambiguity of the modern world, embraced new forms of informal communal activity and harnessed new technology to help them operate in as close to real time as is possible. They have also recognized how the generational shift at the top and bottom of the corporate hierarchy demands a new approach to the way that they manage their people. All of which makes them better equipped to deal with the rapidly changing expectations of employees, customers and other key stakeholders. Being loose won't necessarily make

---

[321] James Dyson interview in *The Times*, 10 October 2009.

them future-proof, but it gives them a chance of responding effectively to what ever the world throws their way.

It is no coincidence that we are witnessing looser forms of community activism and political organization. The Big Society, Tea Party and informal activist movements, such as the Carrotmob, are inevitable responses to a popular frustration with the failure of traditional, tightly controlled ways of achieving social progress. Politicians and activists are often first in line when it comes to spotting new trends, whether using Twitter to reconnect with voters or tapping into people's desire for communal action. Smart businesses will follow their lead and loosen up their thinking, their structures and their procedures. It won't be easy: tight thinking has been in the ascendancy for too long. But when the world's leading financial institutions, economists and business schools start abandoning their long-held rational, empirical viewpoint and start embracing new ideas about real rather than modelled human behaviour, the importance of intuition and critical thinking, there is a sense that the tide is turning in favour of a looser mindset.

Most leaders, if willing to make an honest appraisal, would also accept that the institutions they run have become too slow, too process-bound and too cautious. Why does it take five days to get a press release out of the door? Why are they so poor at their own new product development that they end up having to buy smaller, entrepreneurial businesses to help them enter new markets? Why do endless research studies reveal a high level of managerial frustration at the pace of change within their own organizations? However you choose to look at it, tight most definitely isn't working.

One of the best illustrations of loose in action is improvisational comedy. The true experts at this art form, such as Paul Merton or Eddie Izzard, can link together a bewildering array of unscripted topics into a coherent narrative. Like a jazz group riffing around a theme, they make it look effortless, but it has taken them years of practice to perfect the appearance of sounding completely loose and spontaneous. It is not altogether surprising that some resourceful corporate trainers have started to use improvisational techniques in the workplace. Professor Mary Crosson, a business academic, who made a study of the use of these techniques, has described how, 'We discovered that not only does improvisation provide a way to understand what it takes to be spontaneous and innovative, but exercises used by actors to develop their skill can be adopted by business as a means to experience and enhance individual and organizational capacity to be innovative and responsive.'[322] Eddie Izzard, occasional transvestite and business guru; now that's loose.

[322] Mary Crosson, 'Improvise to Innovate', *Ivey Business Quarterly*, 62, no. 1, 1997.

INDEX

Note: Page numbers in **bold** indicate major text sections. Subscript numbers appended to page numbers indicate a footnote.